Turning Spreadsheets
into Corporate Data

Bill Inmon

Technics Publications

Published by:

2 Lindsley Road
Basking Ridge, NJ 07920 USA

https://www.TechnicsPub.com

Edited by Lauren McCafferty

First Printing 2017
Copyright © 2017 by Bill Inmon

ISBN, print ed.	9781634622288
ISBN, Kindle ed.	9781634621731
ISBN, ePub ed.	9781634621748

Library of Congress Control Number: 2017935502

This book is dedicated to my best friend, Ross Leher-
a pioneer in his own right.

Contents

INTRODUCTION   **1**

1: BRIEF HISTORY OF SPREADSHEETS   **5**

THE IT LABYRINTH   6

END USER ACCEPTANCE OF THE SPREADSHEET   7

SPREADSHEET HELL   8

A TRADEOFF   9

RESPONSIBILITY—THE FLIP SIDE OF CONTROL   10

MANAGEMENT'S PROBLEM   10

DIFFERENCES BETWEEN TWO TYPES OF DATA   11

IN SUMMARY   11

2: SPREADSHEET PARADOX   **13**

PUBLIC DATA   13

THE SPREADSHEET AS A MEDIUM OF EXCHANGE   14

RECURRING/NON-RECURRING SPREADSHEETS   15

THE SPECTRUM OF SPREADSHEETS   16

THE COST OF TRANSFORMING A SPREADSHEET   18

FACTORS OTHER THAN COST   20

TRANSCRIPTION OF DATA   21

CELL FORMULA   21

SPREADSHEET DESCRIPTORS   22

ARTIFICIALLY SUPPLYING DESCRIPTORS   24

IN SUMMARY   24

3: SPREADSHEET VARIETIES   **27**

SIMPLE DEMARCATION—XLSTAB   28

OTHER SPECIAL CHARACTERS—EOLD AND LINEFEED   29

THE INTERNAL VIEW OF A SPREADSHEET   30

A MISSING COLUMN HEADING   31

A MISSING VALUE   32
A MULTILINE ROW   33
THE "STANDARD" SPREADSHEET FORMAT   34
MANAGING THE USER OF THE SPREADSHEET   35
THE SSDEF TABLE   36
THE SPREADSHEET PROCESSING LOG   37
THE LINEAGE OF SPREADSHEET DATA   38
THE CELL FORMULA   39
RELATING TO THE REAL WORLD   39
IDENTIFYING THE HEADER LINE   40
IN SUMMARY   41

4: THE PDF SPREADSHEET   43
THE IMPORTANCE OF SPECIAL CHARACTERS   44
PDF AND OCR   45
A FINAL OPTION   45
IN SUMMARY   46

5: THE BASICS OF SPREADSHEET FORMATTING   47
THE SYSTEM NAME   47
UNRELIABILITY OF REPORT NAME   48
MULTIPLE SHEETS IN A SPREADSHEET   49
OTHER SPECIAL CHARACTERS   49
IDENTIFYING COLUMN HEADINGS   50
SIMILAR COLUMN HEADINGS   50
BLOCKING OFF SECTIONS OF A SPREADSHEET   51
NON-STANDARD SPREADSHEET STRUCTURES   52
A SPREADSHEET THAT CANNOT BE MAPPED   54
A SPREADSHEET IN A TXT FORMAT   54
IN SUMMARY   54

6: SPREADSHEET DISAMBIGUATION   57
SELECTING SPREADSHEETS FOR INCLUSION INTO CORPORATE DATA   57

RECASTING THE SPREADSHEET   59
LOGGING THE SPREADSHEET FOR TRANSFORMATION   59
ENTRY INTO THE PATH QUEUE   60
DEFINING THE SPREADSHEET HEADINGS   60
PAIRING THE SSDEF SPECIFICATION TO THE SPREADSHEET   60
FINDING AND CREATING DATABASE DEFINITIONS AND VALUES   61
THE INTERMEDIATE DATABASE   62
SOME ANOMALIES   62
WHAT IF AN ERROR IS DISCOVERED?   64
MANUAL EFFORT REQUIRED   64
SPREADSHEET WIDTH   65
SUBDIVIDING A SPREADSHEET   65
NO VALUE FOR A COLUMN NAME   66
NO COLUMN HEADINGS   66
CREATING THE SSDEF SPECIFICATION ONCE   66
IN SUMMARY   67

7: THE INTERMEDIATE DATABASE   69
FINDING ERRORS   69
THE CONTENTS OF THE INTERMEDIATE DATABASE   70
FUNCTIONS SERVED BY THE DATA ELEMENTS   71
ALTERNATE NAME   71
ADDING CONTEXT TO DATA VALUES   73
EDITING DATA IN THE INTERMEDIATE DATABASE   73
IN SUMMARY   74

8: THE SSDEF DATABASE   77
ORGANIZING DATA INSIDE THE SSDEF TABLE   77
PROCESSING USING SSDEF RECORDS   78
SEARCHING THE FULL PATH QUEUE   78
IN SUMMARY   79

9: THE CORPORATE DATABASE   81

FROM INTERMEDIATE DATA TO CORPORATE DATA   82
GROUPED CORPORATE DATA   82
TRACING THE LINEAGE   83
IN SUMMARY   83

10: THE MNEMONIC DICTIONARY   85

THE CONTENTS OF THE MNEMONIC DICTIONARY   86
GROUPING LIKE DATA ELEMENTS   86
APPLYING NAMING CONVENTIONS   88
VALUE OF THE MNEMONIC DICTIONARY   88
IN SUMMARY   89

11: POLITICAL CONSIDERATIONS WITHIN THE ORGANIZATION 91

SHIFTING CONTROL   91
IMMUTABILITY OF DATA   92
THE IMPORTANCE OF ALTERNATE NAMES   93
LIMITED EDITING   94
SUPER CLASSIFICATIONS OF DATA   94
THE LINEAGE OF CORPORATE DATA   95
RELATIVE VOLUMES OF DATA   95
IN SUMMARY   95

12: DATA MODELING AND THE SPREADSHEET ENVIRONMENT 97

THE ENTITY RELATIONSHIP DIAGRAM   97
THE DATA ITEM SET   98
THE PHYSICAL MODEL   98
THE DATA MODEL   100
THE DATA MODEL AND SPREADSHEET DATA   100
"CORRECTNESS" OF DATA   101
ALIGNING DATA FROM DIFFERENT SPREADSHEETS   101
AN ALGORITHMIC RESOLUTION   102
AN INDEXED RESOLUTION   102

RESOLUTION AND THE DATA MODEL   103
SPREADSHEET DATA IN THE DATA WAREHOUSE   104
CHANGING SPREADSHEET DATA   105
IN SUMMARY   105

13: CASE STUDY   107

GLOSSARY   113

INDEX   115

Introduction

For years, end users have been longing to take their technological destinies into their own hands. Nearly overnight, the personal computer and the spreadsheet made it entirely possible for the end user to do exactly that. With the personal computer and the spreadsheet, the end user no longer needed IT.

The consequence was an explosion of end user activity. Soon there were personal computers and spreadsheets everywhere. Every end user could be the captain of his or her own ship.

Spreadsheets were created faster and died faster than anyone could hope to keep track of. Spreadsheets were created on whims. Anyone could put anything they wanted in a spreadsheet at any time. The end user was elated at the autonomy that appeared on his doorstep...elated for awhile, at least.

The end user was elated until the end user woke up to find that the data on the spreadsheet was unreliable. Spreadsheets may have been easy to create and update, but making important corporate decisions based on spreadsheets was a risky business for no other reason than the lack of credibility of the data.

Every end user was the captain of his or her own ship—soon there were boats driving all over the ocean, and traffic was so choked that no one ended up going anywhere. There ensued what can be termed "spreadsheet Hell". In spreadsheet Hell, there was no shortage of data, but there was a real drought of credible data.

When it came to making important and potentially risky decisions, management was hesitant to trust the data found on spreadsheets. This was simply because the data on the spreadsheet was so fluid and so flexible that no one really believed it. Any person could change data in a spreadsheet, without authorization or credentials, and there was no tracking process to see what info was changed by what people at what times. Also, the content entered in a spreadsheet cell was rarely validated for correctness or consistency.

Spreadsheets began to play other roles in corporations. Spreadsheets evolved into mediums of data exchange between corporations. When one corporation needed data from another corporation, much of that data was transferred in the form of a spreadsheet. It was much easier to just create a spreadsheet and to send it to the other corporation than it was to sit down and hammer out a formal format for the exchange of data. If the exchange of data was not correct in the case of the spreadsheet, the spreadsheet itself was simply altered.

For these reasons, there comes a time at some point in the technological evolution of a corporation to formalize some of these spreadsheets, so that data coming from them can be more trustworthy and can be relied upon.

Formalizing and introducing discipline in the process of entering data and reading data from a spreadsheet is challenging, but critical. Introducing discipline into the building and usage of spreadsheets is a necessary step in the maturation process of an organization.

This book describes one such process, examining a process that is termed "spreadsheet disambiguation". This book will help you turn spreadsheet data into credible, useful, reliable data that management can trust in order to make important decisions.

One of the most important elements of this book is the concept that values of data are meaningless unless those values are paired with context.

The problem with spreadsheets lies here – spreadsheets are often presented without any context readily apparent. Usually that context is there, but it is elusive. Spreadsheet disambiguation is based on the proposition that in order to have true meaning, there must be both context and values.

Interwoven with the recognition of the importance of context is the notion that lineage of spreadsheet data is of the utmost importance. Because the basis of all spreadsheet data is some person putting numbers on a spreadsheet, lineage becomes vitally important.

Lineage of data has existed since the earliest systems, but it has still managed to play a secondary role in classical corporate systems. In classical corporate systems, the veracity of data – the truthfulness of the values of corporate data – is considered to be of paramount importance. However, when considering spreadsheets, data's lineage is in fact *more* important than its veracity. This is, of course, because the veracity of data relies entirely on the creator of the spreadsheet. For this reason, the lineage of spreadsheet data as it becomes corporate data takes a position of great importance.

This book represents an important step in the maturity of the organization. As corporations mature, they recognize the need to turn some of the data found on spreadsheets into corporate data. And with that comes the need for spreadsheets that are credible and well-organized. Whether you are a manager, developer, end user, or student, this book will help you achieve that state for your spreadsheets and, ultimately, your corporate data.

WHI, Castle Rock, CO May 2017

1: Brief History of Spreadsheets

A long time ago, the IT department ran all aspects of corporate computing. Most computing was done on a large centralized computer. There was a computer budget. There were programmers and analysts. But in short order, this model began to fall apart. Programs, once written, needed to be maintained. End users needed to use a system that was never designed or built with them in mind. Development projects started to take years. The end user was asked to just "wait" until the new system was in place.

And the way systems were developed began to grow more complex and more Byzantine by the day. Users would submit requirements that never resulted in any systems being built. The frustration level grew and never got any better.

The end user was asked to submit his/her requirements into a development process that IT had concocted that could best be described as a labyrinth.

THE IT LABYRINTH

There were massive problems with the labyrinth that had been created by the IT department. Things never got done. Development was an eternal process. The IT department was designated as the controller of the technological destiny of the corporation.

The IT department was forever defining requirements and forever interviewing the end user. The IT department was always drawing curious diagrams that took up whole hallways to display. The IT department was always deep into analysis. The IT department was always running models and struggling with legacy systems. The IT labyrinth had levels and levels of complexity that were understood by no one except some highly-paid guru who seemed to never be available and who spoke in incomprehensible phrases.

The end user was trying to operate in a business environment that was competitive and was ever changing. And the IT organization with its laborious methodologies was a liability, rather than an asset.

It was into this world of frustration and unfulfilled promises that the spreadsheet made its appearance. In many ways the spreadsheet appeared as a lifeline to the end user. The spreadsheet was available and affordable. The spreadsheet did not require a professional programmer to create and manipulate. And, best of all, the spreadsheet could be owned, controlled, and managed without any interference from the IT organization.

For these reasons and many more, the spreadsheet grew in popularity, like flowers in the springtime. Soon spreadsheets were everywhere.

END USER ACCEPTANCE OF THE SPREADSHEET

There were many reasons why the spreadsheet grew in popularity. But at the heart of every reason was the fact that with the spreadsheet, the end user was in control of his or her own destiny. The spreadsheet was the tool that allowed the end user to get out from under the control of the IT organization. And getting out of the control of the IT department meant that things could finally get done. The complicated and involved user requirements that for years had been neglected by the IT department were at last rendered unnecessary.

Furthermore, not only did the end user suddenly have control of data and processing, but with the spreadsheet, data became malleable. New data elements could be added. Data values could be changed. Calculations could be corrected. And all of this flexibility was available with no involvement from the IT department.

Another important factor in the rising popularity of the spreadsheet was transferability. Spreadsheets made it simple to send data from one department to another and from one company to the next. If a company wished to transmit data to another company, the spreadsheet became the default format for the transmission. It was simply expected that a person at the other company would be able to read and interpret the data on a spreadsheet.

In order to transmit data from one organization to another, it's not necessary to engage the IT department. The organization building the spreadsheet simply uses good business sense to construct it. It is expected that that same business sense will be used in the examination and interpretation of the spreadsheet. No predetermined format or database design is required to send a spreadsheet to a business colleague.

For this reason the spreadsheet has become a good way to transmit data from one organization to another.

As important as spreadsheets were and are, they never would have become popular had it not been for the fact that the spreadsheet runs on a personal computer. Personal computers are affordable. There is no blessing of the IT department that is required in order to buy a personal computer. Furthermore, if an individual wants to bring a personal computer into the office, that it strictly up to the individual, not the IT organization.

Because of the affordability and portability of the personal computer, individuals can afford to make the spreadsheet a standard part of the workplace. This same individual could barely even contemplate the purchase of the large mainframes that ran centralized computing "back in the day".

It is because of the personal computer that the spreadsheet is as widespread as it is today.

It is no surprise that spreadsheets became pervasive throughout organizations. Soon spreadsheets were everywhere. The end user had autonomy. The end user had freedom. The end user could create automated data at will.

SPREADSHEET HELL

Then something unexpected happened: spreadsheets became the victims of their own success. Soon there were spreadsheets everywhere. At one Midwestern organization of 3,000 employees, it was estimated that there existed 250,000 spreadsheets. Another issue that arose was the fact that when a spreadsheet was created, that spreadsheet had very limited accessibility. Only the creator of the spreadsheet and perhaps a few other people knew about the existence of the spreadsheet. Because of this limited visibility of data, the same data was being recreated over and over again in different locations by different people. The way the data was created, the calculations, and the edits made to verify the authenticity of the data all were carried out differently. This lack of discipline in managing data further magnified the miseries caused by spreadsheets.

Another problem involved the scope of data that was contained in the spreadsheet. When an end user sat down to create a spreadsheet, the end user typically would look at only the immediate and obvious data. The end user never considered the wide range of people that might be interested in the data. As a result, data found on a spreadsheet had a singularly-focused usage. The fact that other people might have an interest in the data found on the spreadsheet was of no concern to its creator.

The rapid, uncontrolled proliferation of spreadsheets, along with a lack of rigor over their management, led to a condition I lovingly call "Spreadsheet Hell."

A TRADEOFF

Only by going through "Spreadsheet Hell" did the organization learn that there was a tradeoff to be made between end user autonomy and data credibility. The end user could choose to have complete autonomy. But as long as the end user could put any data at any time for any reason on a spreadsheet, then this autonomy became a liability. Just because data was on a spreadsheet did not mean that the data was credible.

Not only was data not believable, but data wasn't reliable. Spreadsheets became lost or corrupted. Backup procedures were nonexistent. Audit procedures were nowhere to be found. Storage procedures and equipment were specious. Making major corporate decisions based on spreadsheet data became a risky endeavor.

RESPONSIBILITY—THE FLIP SIDE OF CONTROL

At the root of the problem was the fact that as long as only the end user could create data, only the end user could be held responsible for the data. The end user – by taking control of their destiny – also assumed responsibility for the accuracy and veracity of the data that arrives on their spreadsheet.

When the end users were finally able to take control, they did not realize that with control came responsibility.

MANAGEMENT'S PROBLEM

"Spreadsheet Hell" put management in a very poor position. All management wanted to do was to make good business decisions. On one hand, the IT department claimed to have rigorously-defined data. The problem was that dealing with IT was a long and tortuous process. When IT took over, there arose the real risk that nothing would ever materialize. The flip side was to let the end user have autonomy of data and processing. Sure enough, things got done. But the net result was not being able to believe the data that decisions were based on.

So management was in a precarious position.

One good solution to this dilemma was to take the data that the end user had manufactured, and to turn that spreadsheet data into corporate data.

Of course, there were risks in this approach. But there are risks in any approach. Whatever management does, there are risks. Doing nothing has its risks. And certainly transforming spreadsheet data to corporate data has its risks.

DIFFERENCES BETWEEN TWO TYPES OF DATA

As data was transformed from spreadsheet data into corporate data, a realization dawned on the corporation. There was a fundamental difference between these two types of data. With spreadsheet data, the lineage of the data could be rigorously defined, but the veracity of the data was questionable. With corporate data, the veracity of the data could be rigorously controlled, but the lineage of the data was unclear.

Not *all* spreadsheets will be or should be transformed into corporate data. It only makes sense that *some* spreadsheets go through the transformation. We will cover which types of spreadsheets should be transformed.

This book is about how to make the transformation of spreadsheet data into corporate data in as orderly and as rational a manner as possible.

IN SUMMARY

Data is at the heart of the decision-making process. Traditionally, data was a byproduct of systems created by IT. But soon, the IT development process became so complicated that the end user looked for a better way to manage data.

Soon the end user stumbled upon the spreadsheet, which was accessible, affordable, and did not require a technician. The spreadsheet allowed the end users to control their own destinies, and thus became very popular.

In fact, the spreadsheet became so popular that the corporate environment became overrun with too many spreadsheets, created by too many people, on whims and without any management. I affectionately refer to this crisis as "Spreadsheet Hell." In "Spreadsheet Hell" there was no shortage of data. But there was a real shortage of believable data.

Management was at a crossroads. They needed to find data that could be used for sound decision making. One way to find this was to take appropriate spreadsheet data and turn it into corporate data.

2: Spreadsheet Paradox

There are many reasons why spreadsheet data needs to be transformed into corporate data, but two reasons stand out among all others. The first of those reasons is the need for credible, publicly shared data. The second reason is the need for more data reliability.

PUBLIC DATA

Suppose a spreadsheet contains data that would be useful in many places throughout the corporation. As long as the spreadsheet remains as a spreadsheet, it will have limited accessibility among the many people in the corporation. Only a few people will know about the spreadsheet. And since the spreadsheet is essentially private, suboptimal care is taken to make sure its values are correct.

In the case of information that is valuable beyond just a few people, there is incentive for the spreadsheet to be transformed into corporate data. And of course, as there evolves a widespread audience using the spreadsheet data, the veracity of the data found on the spreadsheet becomes of great importance.

Usually the places where data is needed publicly are found within the same corporation. Only occasionally is there a need to share spreadsheet data with institutions outside the corporation, when the motivation for transforming the spreadsheet data is to make the spreadsheet data public.

The first motivation, then, for transforming a spreadsheet into corporate data is to greatly increase the audience of people who have access to the data. Once the spreadsheet becomes corporate data, the corporate data is open and available to anyone who needs to examine it. Figure 2.1 illustrates just some of the many different users within a corporation that could benefit from having access to some certain set of public data.

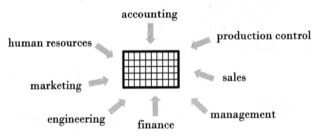

Figure 2.1: Various consumers of public data

THE SPREADSHEET AS A MEDIUM OF EXCHANGE

The second important reason to transform spreadsheet data into corporate data is the need for increased reliability of data as it is transmitted outside the corporate walls. This impetus is very different from the need to make spreadsheet data public.

Spreadsheets have become a natural medium in which to exchange information outside of the corporate walls.

In order to determine which spreadsheets are most appropriate to be transformed into corporate data, it is necessary to understand spreadsheets from a different perspective.

RECURRING/NON-RECURRING SPREADSHEETS

The first way that spreadsheets can be understood is by looking at spreadsheets to see if they are recurring. A non-recurring spreadsheet is one that is created and used only once. It probably is never updated once created. The life of a non-recurring spreadsheet may be as short as a minute. The spreadsheet is created, used for whatever purpose its author intended, and then disposed of or simply filed away, never to be accessed again. There are many forms of non-recurring spreadsheets:

- Grocery lists

- Children to invite to a birthday party

- Calendar of appointments for the next month

- Attendees of a social function

The non-recurring spreadsheet is created, used, and dies—all in a short amount of time. Some non-recurring spreadsheets contain private data. Some non-recurring spreadsheets contain corporate information. In a day's time, the corporation may process thousands of non-recurring spreadsheets that are created and destroyed. In almost every case, the data stored on a non-recurring spreadsheet is informal.

The opposite of a non-recurring spreadsheet is a recurring spreadsheet. A recurring spreadsheet is one that is created and recreated on a regular basis. A typical strategy is to create the spreadsheet on a monthly basis. There can be many types of recurring spreadsheets:

- Monthly revenues for the department

- Monthly expenses for the department

- Monthly vacation time taken by individuals in a department

- Monthly overtime accrued by an individual

Unlike non-recurring spreadsheets, the recurring spreadsheet is periodically updated. One characteristic of recurring spreadsheets is that the recurring spreadsheet can have its format altered from one iteration to the next. The author of the spreadsheet may add a new field of data. The author may move one column around. And – in the mind of the author – it is still the same spreadsheet even though changes may have been made.

There are many ways to characterize the spectrum of spreadsheets. Looking at recurring and non-recurring spreadsheets is only one of many ways. Another way to describe spreadsheets is by considering their formality.

Some spreadsheets are very informal. Other spreadsheets are very formal. A formal spreadsheet is one where the terms are well-defined and the formula associated with those terms are well-defined. An informal spreadsheet is one where there are loosely-defined terms on the spreadsheet and where the formula associated with those terms is fluid and open to interpretation. As a rule, the non-recurring spreadsheets tend to be informal, while the recurring spreadsheets tend to be formal.

THE SPECTRUM OF SPREADSHEETS

Spreadsheets can be arranged on a wide spectrum, starting at very informal non-recurring spreadsheets and ranging to very formal recurring spreadsheets.

When it comes to creating corporate data, the vast majority of spreadsheets do not warrant the care and work that is required to create corporate data. Some of the traits a spreadsheet must have to be a viable candidate for corporate data include:

- The spreadsheet is formal, rather than informal

- The spreadsheet is recurring

- The data on the spreadsheet is useful to a large audience

Examples include spreadsheets that will be used for inter-corporate communication and transferability of data.

Figure 2.2 shows which portion of spreadsheets may be good candidates to be turned into corporate data.

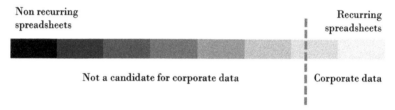

Figure 2.2: Only a portion of spreadsheets are good candidates to be turned into corporate data

The transformation of spreadsheets for the purpose of creating internal corporate data (called public data), is a little different than the case of creating corporate data out of recurring spreadsheets for the purpose of intercompany communication.

When you look at the spectrum of transforming spreadsheets into public data, the candidates for transformation look quite a bit different than the candidates for transformation for the purpose of intercompany communication.

This difference occurs because public data has a wide audience and intercompany communication has the role of communication. As an analogy, consider the work done by an accounting firm. The accounting firm prepares one set of data for internal use within the company and another set of data for filings with the IRS.

Figure 2.3 shows that a few spreadsheets found in various parts of the company are candidates for this kind of transformation. The candidates for this kind of transformation are very different from the candidates for other kinds of transformations. The characteristics for the occasional spreadsheet are that it is used by different organizations. It does not have to be (but can be) either formal or recurring.

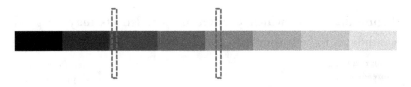

Figure 2.3: Only a few spreadsheets are candidates for transformation

THE COST OF TRANSFORMING A SPREADSHEET

Making the transformation from spreadsheet to corporate data can be achieved in a variety of ways. One way the data can be transformed is manually. It is possible to read a spreadsheet manually, strip off the data that is desired, and then place the data into a database. There is great appeal to the manual approach. It can be done immediately; all that is required is a little bit of training. No great investment is required. And as long as there aren't too many spreadsheets and as long as the spreadsheets are not too complicated, the manual approach works just fine.

But what if there are a lot of spreadsheets? The manual approach quickly breaks down. Using the manual approach:

- There is the ongoing cost of human involvement. Humans cost a lot.

- There is the fatigue factor. The quality of human work deteriorates over time.

- There is the mistake factor. Humans make mistakes.

- There is the speed factor. Humans can only work so fast.

In short, while the low initial investment makes the manual approach attractive, in the face of lots of spreadsheets, the manual approach quickly becomes a burdensome way to proceed.

The alternative to the manual creation of corporate data from spreadsheet data is, of course, the automated process. Just as with the manual method, though, there are several obstacles to the automated creation of corporate data from spreadsheet data.

The first obstacle is complexity. Instead of having a human who can absorb instructions as to what to look for how to treat data, the analyst must teach computers how to do the same thing. Teaching computers is much more complicated than teaching humans the same thing. Furthermore, specialized technology is required for accomplishing the transformation.

For these reasons, there is an obstacle to overcome when starting any corporate data transformation. There is no question that it is faster and simpler to start the transformation manually rather than through automation.

But the costs of transformation go up exponentially as you continue to do the work manually, increasing in cost as the number of spreadsheets increases. When faced with a great quantity of spreadsheets, the ongoing costs of manual transformation far exceed any startup savings. Figure 2.4 illustrates these cost differentials when there are few spreadsheets involved.

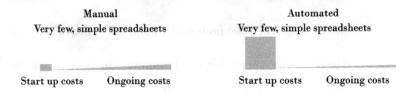

Figure 2.4: Manual vs Automated when only a few spreadsheets

But if there are lots of spreadsheets to be transformed, then the difference in the startup costs are mitigated by the ongoing costs of having to do the transformation manually. Figure 2.5 illustrates how different the costs are when you have many complex spreadsheets.

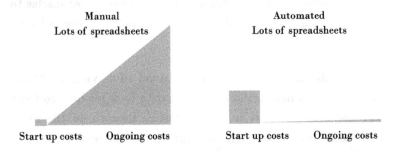

Figure 2.5: Manual vs automated processing when many spreadsheets are involved

FACTORS OTHER THAN COST

Cost is important, but it is not the only factor that will determine the best way to transform spreadsheets into corporate data. Accuracy and time must also be taken into consideration. For example, a spreadsheet that takes 30 days to process manually could be automatically processed in a matter of seconds.

The other major factor is the accuracy of transformation. Humans make errors for a variety of reasons. It is reasonable to expect a 70% to 80% accuracy rate in transforming spreadsheets manually. However, when transforming spreadsheets in an automated manner, it is reasonable to expect a 100% accuracy rate.

TRANSCRIPTION OF DATA

Now that we've discussed the two ways in which data can be transformed, let's dive into the basics of the work that must be done to get from a spreadsheet to corporate data. There are actually many steps in this process. But the most basic concepts are the transcription and interpretation of the data.

Transcription of data is the easy part. A cell has a value. The cell is identified and the value is lifted. It is a mechanical process. The more challenging thing about reading and interpreting a spreadsheet is taking into account the context of the data.

CELL FORMULA

In the simple spreadsheet represented by Figure 2.6, the value of the highlighted cell is "7". The number "7" by itself is "naked". In fact *any* number, by itself, is "naked". In order for the number "7" to have any meaning, the number requires context.

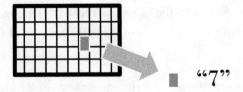

Figure 2.6: When you look at a cell of data, there is nothing that tells you what that cell of data represents

And there is context – of sorts – associated with the number "7" in the spreadsheet. Every cell in a spreadsheet has an underlying formula. For example, the cell with the number "7" may have the underlying formula "A1 + C3 / B5". This descriptive data would mean that the value of "7" was calculated by taking the contents of cell A1 and adding the contents of cell C3, then dividing the result by the contents of cell B5. This could be considered some context that *is* found within the spreadsheet itself.

But that's not much meaningful information. The spreadsheet formula does not really describe what is going on. There are *much* more meaningful ways to describe the meaning of the contents of a cell than to declare that its formula has meaning.

SPREADSHEET DESCRIPTORS

A much better way to understand the meaning of a cell is to look and see what descriptors are to be found on the spreadsheet itself. As a rule, a cell often has a column heading and a row identifier associated with the cell, as shown in Figure 2.7.

There are, however, some basic problems with identifying a cell by its column name and its row identifier. The first problem is that column name and row identification are optional descriptors. The analyst creating the spreadsheet may not have created one or the other (or both!) of these forms of metadata.

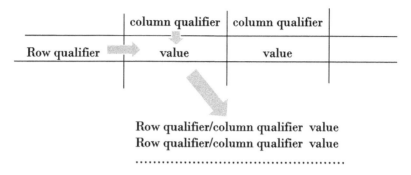

	column qualifier	column qualifier	
Row qualifier	value	value	

Row qualifier/column qualifier value
Row qualifier/column qualifier value

Figure 2.7: One column and one row point to one cell

But even if the analyst has created both the column name and the row identifier, aligning the two can be a challenge. In a spreadsheet it is easy to access an entire column, thus making the association between the column name and the values in the column obvious. Or it is easy to simply access row of data, thereby making the association between the row identifier and the value of data in the cell obvious.

What is more challenging is to marry both the row identifier *and* the column name to the value of data. However, when the row identifier and the column name are married together, they serve as a good way to attach meaning to a cell value in a spreadsheet.

The essence of spreadsheets is a free-form collection of data. There is *nothing* in spreadsheet technology that requires that a person create both a column heading and a row identifier. However, in the case of more formally designed spreadsheets, it is common to find both column name and row identifiers. This is one reason why more formal spreadsheets make good candidates to be turned into corporate data.

ARTIFICIALLY SUPPLYING DESCRIPTORS

It is always possible to artificially supply column names and row identifiers to spreadsheet data. But the artificial application of this data is tedious and laborious, and is usually not worth the effort. However, at least technically speaking, an artificial application of both column name and row identifier is possible (if impractical).

However it is accomplished, if data is going to be sent from a spreadsheet to corporate data, there must exist two elements: context and value.

IN SUMMARY

Spreadsheets serve a wide variety of purposes. Two of the purposes they serve are for storage of valuable data, and for exchanging data between different entities. It is in these two roles that spreadsheets are often cast into the form of corporate data.

Spreadsheets can be characterized in many ways. One way to characterize spreadsheets is on a spectrum of non-recurring spreadsheets to recurring spreadsheets. As a rule, the more recurring the spreadsheet is, the more formal it is.

In terms of selecting spreadsheets for a basis for corporate data, the more formal and the more recurring a spreadsheet is, the more likely that the spreadsheet be transformed into corporate data.

In order to change spreadsheet data into corporate data, it is necessary to have both value and context. The best way to find the context of data found on a spreadsheet is to identify the column name and the row identifier of a value. Unfortunately, the cell formula found in a spreadsheet is of little value in determining context.

A column name and/or a row identifier can artificially be assigned to data from a spreadsheet. However, the artificial assignment of this information is usually not very practical.

3: Spreadsheet Varieties

In order to understand how spreadsheet data can be turned into corporate data, we must understand spreadsheets at two levels. The first level can be called the "external" level. The external level of a spreadsheet is the way a spreadsheet looks to the user. When you look at a spreadsheet on the desk or on the computer, you are looking at it "externally."

The other way a spreadsheet can be examined or understood is "internally". Almost no one sees this internal view, except for the computer. The spreadsheet looks very different to the computer than it looks to the end user or the analyst.

The reason why it is important to understand what a spreadsheet looks like internally is because the internal view determines much of what can and cannot be accomplished with the data. In order to turn spreadsheet data into corporate data, you need to understand what is happening and why it is happening. Figure 3.1 illustrates these two views (or levels) of a spreadsheet.

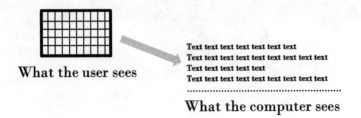

Figure 3.1: External and internal views

Indeed, the internal view of what a computer sees depends *entirely* on which spreadsheet technology is being used to create and manage the spreadsheet. The internal view of a Microsoft Excel® spreadsheet will probably look entirely different from the internal view of another spreadsheet. Furthermore, it is entirely possible that different versions of Excel may use different internal formats.

It is fair to say that Microsoft's Excel technology dominates the marketplace. For this reason, Microsoft's Excel technology will be used throughout this book. Keep in mind, though, that there exist other spreadsheet technologies with their own internal formats and conventions.

SIMPLE DEMARCATION—XLSTAB

In its simplest form, the Microsoft Excel technology has an internal format where a value is delimited from another value by the appearance of a special character called the "xlstab" character. The xlstab character is Hex 0x09. When you read a spreadsheet internally, the values are separated by the xlstab character.

Figure 3.2 shows the xlstab character and its positioning.

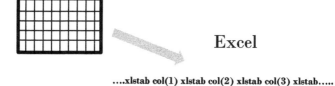

....xlstab col(1) xlstab col(2) xlstab col(3) xlstab.....

Figure 3.2: The generic internal format for Excel

OTHER SPECIAL CHARACTERS—EOLD AND LINEFEED

Two other important special characters found in an internal spreadsheet are the end of line (or *eold*) character and the *linefeed* character. The eold character is Hex 0x0D and the linefeed character is Hex 0x0A.

The eold and linefeed characters demark the beginning of a new line and the ending of an old line, respectively. Between the eold, linefeed, and xstab characters, the internal structure of a spreadsheet can be easily understood.

Figure 3.3 shows how the eold, linefeed, and xlstab characters appear in the internal view of a spreadsheet.

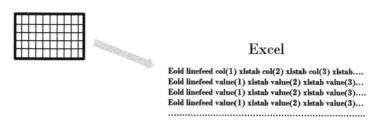

Excel

Eold linefeed col(1) xlstab col(2) xlstab col(3) xlstab....
Eold linefeed value(1) xlstab value(2) xlstab value(3)...
Eold linefeed value(1) xlstab value(2) xlstab value(3)....
Eold linefeed value(1) xlstab value(2) xlstab value(3)...
....

Figure 3.3: The generic internal format for Excel with line control

In short, the internal view of a spreadsheet consists of the values found on the spreadsheet and a few special characters.

When you are approaching a transformation from a spreadsheet to corporate data, it is *always* wise to first check and see what special characters are being used internally by your spreadsheet software. If you attempt a transformation from a spreadsheet to a corporate database and you are using a different set of special characters than what you expect to be using, you won't be able to make the transformation either properly or at all.

For that reason alone, when you begin a spreadsheet to corporate database transformation, *always* check and make sure you know what the internal structuring of the spreadsheet looks like.

It is easy to ascertain what the internal structure of the spreadsheet looks like. This can be done by converting the spreadsheet to a .txt format then looking at the spreadsheet as a .txt document.

THE INTERNAL VIEW OF A SPREADSHEET

So what does a "normal" spreadsheet look like internally? Figure 3.4 shows an example.

	Col(1)	Col(2)	Col(3)	
Row id(1)	value	value	value	
Row id(2)	value	value	value	
Row id(3)	value	value	value	
....	....	....	....	

Eold linefeed xlstab col(1) xlstab col(2) xlstab col(3)
Eold linefeed row id(1) xlstab value xlstab value xlstab value
Eold linefeed row id(2) xlstab value xlstab value xlstab value
Eold linefeed row id(3) xlstab value xlstab value xlstab value
....

Figure 3.4: The external and the internal view of a sample spreadsheet

The first internal line of data after the eold and linefeed character begins with an xlstab character. This means that the first column of the first row is blank. Then comes the information about the first column definition: "col(1)". Then comes another xlstab. This demarks the end of the column and the start of the next column. This is followed by the information about column number two: "col(2)". Next comes an xlstab which demarks the end of the second column and the start of the third column. Next comes the information about the third column: "col(3)".

That information is followed by the eold and the linefeed character. This demarks the end of column three and the start of the next line. The second line starts with the information about the first row, which begins with row identifier(1). This is followed by xlstab which signals the end of row identifier(1) and the start of the first value. The first value is followed by an xlstab.

The internal formatting of the rest of the spreadsheet follows in the same manner. Unfortunately, not all spreadsheets are "normal." Let's consider the internal views of some spreadsheets with odd circumstances.

A MISSING COLUMN HEADING

Consider the simple spreadsheet seen in Figure 3.5. As you can see, there is no definition for the second column heading. The second column heading is blank.

The first line of the internal definition is the same as the internal view seen in Figure 3.5, except there is no col(2) information. The internal view of this new spreadsheet would look like: "col(1) xlstab xlstab col(3) xlstab".

	Col(1)		Col(3)
Row id(1)	value	value	value
Row id(2)	value	value	value
Row id(3)	value	value	value

```
Eold linefeed xlstab col(1) xlstab xlstab col(3)
Eold linefeed row id(1) xlstab value xlstab value xlstab value
Eold linefeed row id(2) xlstab value xlstab value xlstab value
Eold linefeed row id(3) xlstab value xlstab value xlstab value
```

Figure 3.5: The external and the internal view of a spreadsheet where one of the column headings is not present

A MISSING VALUE

Now consider a different variation of the same spreadsheet - a spreadsheet with one of the values missing. Figure 3.6 shows the same spreadsheet but with the value in row 2/line 3 omitted.

	Col(1)	Col(2)	Col(3)	
Row id(1)	value	value	value	
Row id(2)	value		value	
Row id(3)	value	value	value	

```
Eold linefeed xlstab col(1) xlstab xlstab col(3)
Eold linefeed row id(1) xlstab value xlstab value xlstab value
Eold linefeed row id(2) xlstab value xlstab xlstab value
Eold linefeed row id(3) xlstab value xlstab value xlstab value
```

Figure 3.6: The external and the internal view of a spreadsheet where one of the values is not present

The result is that row 2/line 3 reads "eold linefeed row id(2) xlstab value xlstab xlstab value". The interpretation of that line is that there is a value for column 1 and for column 3, but not for column 2.

A MULTILINE ROW

For another variation, consider the case of the multiline row. In a multiline row, the analyst has specified that the same row identifier applies to more than one line. In the case of the example shown in Figure 3.7, there are a total of three rows that fall under the same row identifier.

	Col(1)	Col(2)	Col(3)
Row id(1)	value	value	value
	value	value	value
	value	value	value
Row id (2)	value	value	value
	value	value	value
	value	value	value

```
Eold linefeed xlstab col(1) xlstab col(2) xlstab col(3)
Eold linefeed row id(1) xlstab value xlstab value xlstab value
Eold linefeed xlstab value xlstab value xlstab value
Eold linefeed xlstab value xlstab value xlstab value
Eold linefeed row id(2) xlstab value xlstab value xlstab value
Eold linefeed xlstab value xlstab value xlstab value
Eold linefeed xlstab value xlstab value xlstab value
```

Figure 3.7: The external and the internal view of a spreadsheet where multiline values are specified

The internal view of the first row identifier looks the same as it does in the example shown in Figure 3.4. But the second row in the multiline spreadsheet will be different: "eold linefeed xlstab value xlstab value xlstab value".

In order to manipulate a spreadsheet, the analyst must operate confidently at the internal level. The analyst must understand the meaning of the special characters and their structure in order to be able to correctly interpret the spreadsheet.

The importance of the ability to understand spreadsheets internally cannot be understated. It is only at the internal level that a connection can be made between a value and its relevant context. In order to understand a spreadsheet, you must know the column name and row identifier that relate to a value. The column name and the row identifier are the context that bring life to the values found on a spreadsheet.

THE "STANDARD" SPREADSHEET FORMAT

The end user can format a spreadsheet any way they wish. For that reason, there are no official (or even unofficial) ways to format a spreadsheet. However, when considering a spreadsheet for the purpose of corporate data, there must be a "standard" spreadsheet format.

Spreadsheets that are most likely to form the basis of corporate data are those spreadsheets that are formal. Some amount of thought has gone into these more formalized spreadsheets. Really informal spreadsheets seldom make good candidates for corporate data—they may have no headings or even row identifiers. Whoever created the more formal spreadsheets did so under the assumption that it is more than one person was going to utilize the spreadsheet.

For these reasons, then, any spreadsheet that is a viable candidate for corporate data must be in some standard format. The ideal "standard" format of a spreadsheet is seen in Figure 3.8. This standard spreadsheet format consists of at least one column heading and rows of data where each row has a row identifier. An alternative form of a standard spreadsheet is one where the row identifier has its own column heading.

	Col(1)	Col(2)	Col(3)
Row id(1)	value	value	value
Row id(2)	value	value	value
Row id(3)	value	value	value

....

Figure 3.8: Standard format for a corporate data spreadsheet

MANAGING THE USER OF THE SPREADSHEET

Now suppose the organization is gathering spreadsheets, and the end user community submits those spreadsheets for inclusion into corporate data. Suppose the end user community objects to having to comply with a standard spreadsheet format. After all, the end user community argues that the world of spreadsheets is a freeform, uncontrolled world, and the end user can do anything the end user wants.

Such an attitude is entirely within the realm of reasonability, as the end user community has never before been subjected to discipline and rigor when it comes to the subject of spreadsheet structure.

A good rejoinder to this attitude is that the end user is free to submit whatever spreadsheets that he or she wants to. However, because it will take the analyst considerable time and effort to reformat these spreadsheets into the standard form, a processing fee will apply.

Another approach is to "publish" the specifications for what the format of a spreadsheet should look like to be included in a corporate data transformation. In many cases the end user is more than happy to cooperate and to place the spreadsheet into an acceptable format.

There are several reasons why the standard format is a precursor to successful transformation of spreadsheets into a corporate database. Again, the standard format ensures that the values found on the spreadsheet have proper context – column names and row identifiers. Without this context, the system cannot distinguish a line of columns from a row of data. When you are looking at an internal view of a row of data, unless someone or something tells you where the line of column names is, you won't be able to tell what is data and what is metadata. Therefore it is absolutely mandatory that a column of spreadsheet data be identified before the spreadsheet can be transformed into corporate data.

Note that the standard spreadsheet format does not prohibit multiple columnar lines on a spreadsheet. For example, rows 1through10 of a spreadsheet may be defined by the column headings found on row 1. But on row 11, there may be a different set of column headings that define rows 12 -20. There must be at least one line of column headings, but there may be more than one line of columnar headings.

THE SSDEF TABLE

Once the standard format for the spreadsheet is determined, the standard format is defined to a database known as the "ssdef" database. The ssdef database is a system database used in the processing of spreadsheets in the transformation into corporate data. The ssdef database doesn't have much use outside of this process.

The ssdef database is the library of spreadsheet heading definitions that will be transformed into corporate data. The ssdef database is created by stripping off the heading columns of the standard spreadsheet and placing the column headings into the sdef database.

THE SPREADSHEET PROCESSING LOG

Another important component in the transformation process is the log that is created when a spreadsheet arrives to be processed. This log keeps track of which spreadsheets have been submitted for transformation processing. Every spreadsheet that is to be processed is "logged in."

The reason why the logging in of spreadsheets to be transformed is important is that the log forms an essential part of what is called the *lineage* of spreadsheet data.

The transformation log contains some basic information, including:

- The spreadsheet name

- The source of the spreadsheet

- The date and time the spreadsheet was submitted

- By whom the spreadsheet was submitted

THE LINEAGE OF SPREADSHEET DATA

One of the most important features of spreadsheet data is its lineage. The lineage of spreadsheet data includes the record of where the spreadsheet data came from, the processing that it was subjected to, and the final transition into corporate data. There must always be a careful and formal log of the lineage of spreadsheet data.

There is a reason why lineage of spreadsheet data is important. Spreadsheet data is different from other "standard" corporate data. In "standard" corporate data (typically transaction based data), great care is taken to ensure the accuracy of the data. And if "standard" corporate data is shown to be wrong (have an incorrect value), then corrections are made to the standard data.

But spreadsheet data is different. At the root of every value found in spreadsheet data is a person who placed the data there. Only that person knows if the data on the spreadsheet is accurate or not, and only the owner of the spreadsheet can go back and change the data.

Therefore, when the source of data is a spreadsheet, the lineage of the spreadsheet data becomes very important. If corporate data is ever questioned, then there must be a quick and straightforward way to go back to the original owner of the source spreadsheet and determine whether the data is correct.

Typically the lineage of spreadsheet data includes:

- The spreadsheet itself

- The log of the spreadsheet

- Logic for spreadsheet disambiguation

- ssdef table

- Logic to transform into corporate data

THE CELL FORMULA

One of the most basic parts of the lineage of spreadsheet data is the cell metadata (or cell formula) that exists for every cell in the spreadsheet. Figure 3.9 shows an example of cell metadata.

While cell metadata is an interesting feature, it has limited use. The main problem with cell metadata is that it doesn't relate *directly* to the real world. A cell formula tells only what the cell relates to *inside* the spreadsheet. The cell formula does not describe how the cell relates to the real world, *outside* the spreadsheet.

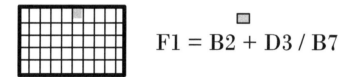

$$F1 = B2 + D3 / B7$$

Figure 3.9: Cell metadata

RELATING TO THE REAL WORLD

If the cell formula cannot define the relationship of a cell to the real world, something else must. This context is provided by the cell's column name and row identifier.

A convenient way to think of this contextual data is as a telescopic sight on a hunting rifle. One hair of the telescopic sight is the column name and the other hair in the telescopic sight is the row identifier. Those two parameters work together to define the context of the value being sighted, as shown in Figure 3.10.

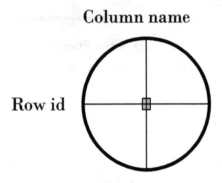

Figure 3.10: Using row id and column name puts the value in the crosshairs

When transforming a spreadsheet into corporate data, it is desirable to make the process as streamlined and as automated as possible. Future chapters on spreadsheet disambiguation will outline the work that needs to be done here.

IDENTIFYING THE HEADER LINE

There is one inescapable chore that *must* be done manually: the identification of a header line versus a data line (or a row of data that contains a row identifier and values). There is no internal difference between these two types of lines.

For this reason, there *must* be manual intervention involved in spreadsheet disambiguation.

Sure, ideally, spreadsheet disambiguation should be free of manual intervention.

But it is a specious argument to say that something as manual as the creation of a spreadsheet should be completely automated. If complete automation was required, then a spreadsheet should never have been used in the first place. Fortunately, this process of identifying headers is quickly accomplished, taking just a few seconds.

IN SUMMARY

Spreadsheets can be understood at two levels: an external level and an internal level. It is necessary to understand spreadsheets at the internal level in order to grasp the scope of what kind of data analysis is possible.

There are three special characters that are found at the internal level: xlstab, linefeed, and eold. The spreadsheet as defined by the user is translated into a string of text that is formatted with the content of the spreadsheet.

Spreadsheets can and should be formatted by the end user in a "standard" format. Once the spreadsheet has been formatted as such, it can be converted into a corporate database.

In order to be converted into a corporate database, each value must have context. Context is determined by the intersection of the column name and the row identifier.

The row containing column names is identified manually by the end user and placed in a database called the ssdef table. A spreadsheet can have multiple column names, but must have at least one line of column headings.

As a spreadsheet arrives for processing, it is logged into a user-managed log. The log is important because it plays a role in the lineage of the spreadsheet data.

The lineage of spreadsheet data is important because it allows all the data to be traced back to its original source. This can be vital if there is ever a question of its accuracy.

4: The PDF Spreadsheet

Spreadsheets are usually created in a Microsoft Excel (.xls) format. There are a lot of advantages to creating, transporting, and using the spreadsheet in that format. The primary advantage of spreadsheets in the .xls format is one of universal understanding. The second advantage is the xlstab control characters are not lost when looking at a spreadsheet as an .xls document.

But people frequently use the Adobe .pdf format to read and transport the .xls spreadsheet. Many think that more convenient to save or store the spreadsheet in a .pdf format.

For most purposes, storing the spreadsheet in a .pdf format is acceptable. But for the purpose of transforming the spreadsheet into corporate data, the .pdf formatting of a spreadsheet is not ideal.

The reason why .pdf spreadsheets are not very helpful for creating corporate data is fairly straightforward. Remember that when a spreadsheet is stored in an .xls format, it contains an internal view including special characters such as xlstab, linefeed, and eold. You may not be able to see these special characters from the external view, but they're still there.

When the same spreadsheet is stored in a .pdf format, you're only seeing the external view of the spreadsheet. The .pdf rendering is an image that has been created by "taking a snapshot" of the spreadsheet.

When a spreadsheet is stored in a .pdf format, it has the same external view of the spreadsheet as stored in an .xls format. However, all that is in the .pdf image is what is seen on the screen. It has no internal view. Therefore, it has no special characters.

THE IMPORTANCE OF SPECIAL CHARACTERS

There are some serious consequences of this lack of special characters in the .pdf spreadsheet. In the .xls format, it is because of the xlstab special character that the alignment of columns can be precisely determined. And because the alignment of the columns can be determined, the context of the values in the spreadsheet can be determined. Again, it is absolutely mandatory that the context of the values on the spreadsheet be determined in order to move the spreadsheet data to the corporate database.

So the loss of special characters in the .pdf format has dire consequences for turning spreadsheet data into corporate data.

Does this mean that spreadsheets should *never* be placed into a .pdf image format? Well, if the spreadsheet is going to be used as corporate data, probably not. If at all possible, keep the spreadsheet out of a .pdf format.

However, if the spreadsheet has already been placed into a .pdf format, all is not lost. There are steps you can take to compensate for the shortcomings of the .pdf formatting.

PDF AND OCR

One alternative is to subject the .pdf image to OCR (optical character recognition) technology. This way, you can read the contents of the spreadsheet on a line-by-line basis.

The best time to turn the OCR option on is during the initial capture of the spreadsheet. However, even if the OCR option was not on when the spreadsheet was initially captured, it is always possible to go back and turn the OCR option on after the fact.

Again, OCR reads and records the spreadsheet, allowing you to identify the row identifiers. However, you still have lost the column names. Without the xlstab characters, it is *very* difficult to determine what the column names are.

A FINAL OPTION

If your .pdf is not available in any other format, as a last resort, you can try to infer the column name headings by using a double blank as a delimiter. This is demonstrated in Figure 4.1.

Once the OCR option has been used, the column headings are there.

So what are the problems with using a double blank as a delimiter? There are lots of problems. The first problem is reliability. In some cases it will not be obvious which values are applicable to which column headings.

Linefeedbᴠalueb̶b̶b̶ᴠaluebb̶b̶b̶ᴠaluebbb̶b̶ᴠalue........

b̶ Equals blank

Figure 4.1: What a line of a spreadsheet looks like after passing through a .pdf rendering

The second problem is that a double blank is not always reliable. In the case of a long column name there may be no double blank. The third problem is that in some cases there may be more blanks than a double blank that separates column names. Clearly, there are some really messy problems that are associated with trying to delineate column names in a .pdf format.

IN SUMMARY

People sometimes place a spreadsheet into Adobe .pdf format. As long as the spreadsheet is not being used for corporate data, using this .pdf format works just fine. However, for transforming the spreadsheet into corporate data, it is best to keep the spreadsheet in its native format.

The key reason why .pdf formatting is not ideal is that the special characters at the internal level of the spreadsheet are lost when the spreadsheet is rendered as a .pdf.

The .pdf rendering of data is essentially a snapshot of the spreadsheet. Even turning the OCR option on does not bring back the hidden special characters.

5: The Basics of Spreadsheet Formatting

In order for a spreadsheet to be transformed into corporate data, it is necessary to understand some basic concepts and terminology about a spreadsheet.

THE SYSTEM NAME

There is only one reliable unique identifier for a spreadsheet: the system name. The system name is the name the spreadsheet is known as to the system. Every document in the system has some name. Some system names are long and cryptic. Other system names are short and simple.

For example, the name inside the system would be the name of the directory the spreadsheet is found in, the folder name (or names if there are multiple folders), and the designated system name. The system name inside the computer might look like this: C:\poc\alba071-investor-eport-dec-07-amended.xlsx.

But even the system name of the spreadsheet may be unreliable. It is easily possible that the spreadsheet was accessed at 10:06 a.m. using the system name. Then at 10:32 a.m., the owner of the spreadsheet changed the spreadsheet inside the system, but did not give it a new name. So at 11:13 a.m. when the system name is accessed again, it is actually a different spreadsheet.

However, for the purposes of this book, it will be assumed that the system identifier of a spreadsheet is unique and reliable.

UNRELIABILITY OF REPORT NAME

It is tempting to say that the spreadsheet name is a reliable identifier of the spreadsheet. While it may well be true that a spreadsheet does have a unique report name on the spreadsheet, ANY data found on the spreadsheet is not reliable. That is because any data found on the spreadsheet is subject to the whims of the author of the report. And there are a thousand reasons why the author may have gotten the report name on the spreadsheet incorrect:

- The report name was misspelled.

- The report name was forgotten.

- The author knew the report name but forgot to put the report name on the spreadsheet.

- The author was confused.

Any one of those reasons leads to an unreliable report name, which should not be used as an identifier. So for purposes of identification, the system spreadsheet name is the one that is used.

MULTIPLE SHEETS IN A SPREADSHEET

One of the factors that must be taken into consideration is that the report name as the spreadsheet is known to the system may actually contain multiple sheets, similar to how a book contains multiple pages.

Figure 5.1 shows that a spreadsheet may consist of multiple "sheets".

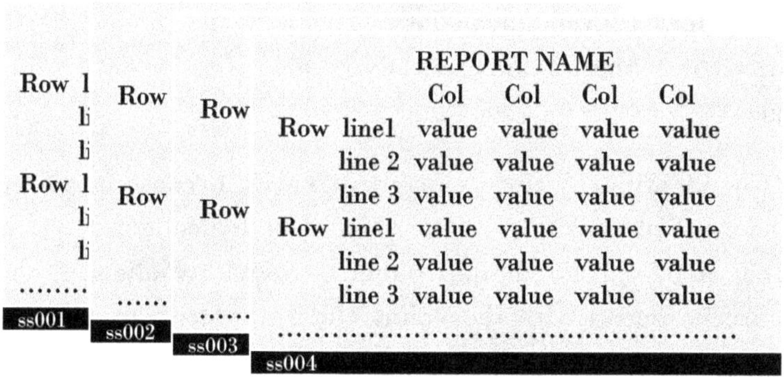

Figure 5.1: A "book" of spreadsheets

OTHER SPECIAL CHARACTERS

The special characters that have been discussed so far include xlstab, linefeed, and eold. But there are lots of other features and types of special characters that can be encountered when looking at a spreadsheet. A spreadsheet may contain, for instance:

- Graphics

- Photos

- Colors

While these features of spreadsheets are interesting, for the purpose of the transformation to corporate data, they are essentially ignored. Corporate data is built upon the very basic constructs of the spreadsheet when a transformation is made.

IDENTIFYING COLUMN HEADINGS

As already discussed, the heart of creating corporate data from spreadsheets is the ability to identify meaningful context of values placed on the spreadsheet. The way this is done is to identify the column name and the row identifier for each value of data.

The row identifier is always easy to identify because it resides on the same physical line as the value. But the column name is another matter. The column name is found by aligning the xlstab occurrences with the value. But in order to even know that a column line signifies a column, the system must learn which line contains the column headings. As mentioned earlier, this can only be achieved manually, by entering the column heading line into the ssdef table.

SIMILAR COLUMN HEADINGS

What if two column headings are very similar, but still have slight differences? This is a very common circumstance. Consider when an analyst submits a spreadsheet for the month of May.

The column headings are captured into an ssdef table. Now for the month of June, the analyst adds a simple column. Out of a large spreadsheet containing many values, only one new value has been added.

Is the definition of the columns as created in May going to be able to be used for the month of June? The answer is no. If definitions of column headings are to be reused, they must be *exact* matches.

Now suppose the analyst has defined column headings for the month of August to the system in the ssdef table. However, there is no new data to report in September, so the analyst simply reuses the same spreadsheet from August. Will the header lines that were defined in August still work for the month of September? Because there have been no changes to the spreadsheet, yes.

BLOCKING OFF SECTIONS OF A SPREADSHEET

On occasion, a spreadsheet is used for a report. Whole blocks of the spreadsheet are used for reporting, not spreadsheet analysis. On those occasions it is possible to block out whole sections of the spreadsheet.

The blocking goes from line n to line n+m. There can be more than one section of the spreadsheet blocked out if necessary. When the system encounters a section of the spreadsheet to be blocked out, the section is essentially removed from the spreadsheet.

Figure 5.2 shows the blocking of major sections of the spreadsheet.

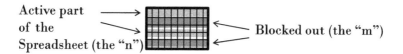

Figure 5.2: If desired whole sections of the spreadsheet can be "blocked out"

NON-STANDARD SPREADSHEET STRUCTURES

We've described in detail the optimal "standard" spreadsheet structure. Again, if you plan to use a spreadsheet to create corporate data, it is ideal to use this "standard" structure as we've described it. However, we must consider another very common spreadsheet structure: a simple list of values, as demonstrated in Figure 5.3.

Row id(1)	value
Row id(2)	value
Row id(3)	value
Row id(4)	value
Row id(5)	value

Figure 5.3: A simple list

The simple list is very common – so much so that it needs to be recognized just like the "standard" format is recognized.

There is one very significant difference between the standard format and the simple list: the determination of the context of values. With the standard format, the context of value is given by a combination of the column name and row identifier. For a simple list, though, the context is often exclusively found in the row identifier. Figure 5.4 shows what a simple list looks like at the internal spreadsheet level.

Eold linefeed row id(1) xlstab value
Eold linefeed row id(2) xlstab value
Eold linefeed row id(3) xlstab value
Eold linefeed row id(4) xlstab value
Eold linefeed row id(5) xlstab value

Figure 5.4: What the simple list looks like at the internal spreadsheet level

An interesting question arises. If spreadsheet disambiguation involves reading the internal structure of a spreadsheet, how can this process tell the difference between a line preceded by a column name and a simple list? The answer is that the spreadsheet disambiguation technology reads the number of xlstab's found in a line. When there exist more than one xlstab in a line, the line must not be part of a simple list. This is illustrated in Figure 5.5, which directly compares the "standard" structure with the simple list structure.

	Col	Col	Col	
Row id	value	value	value	
Row id	value	value	value	
Row id	value	value	value	
....	....	....	....	
Row id	value			
Row id	value			
Row id	value			
....	......			
....	....			

Figure 5.5: A standard spreadsheet format is changed into a simple list format within the same spreadsheet

Figure 5.6 shows an internal view of the spreadsheet depicted in Figure 5.5. It clearly shows the difference between lines of data superseded by a column heading and rows of data in a simple list.

```
Eold linefeed xlstab col xlstab col xlstab col
Eold linefeed row id xlstab value xlstab value xlstab value
Eold linefeed rowid xlstab value xlstab value xlstab value
Eold linefeed rowid xlstab value xlstab value xlstab value
Eold linefeed
Eold linefeed
Eold linefeed row id xlstab value
Eold linefeed row id xlstab value
Eold linefeed row id xlstab value
....................................................
```

Figure 5.6: You can tell the difference between a standard format and a simple list by counting the number of xlstab characters in the line

A Spreadsheet that Cannot be Mapped

Given what we know about the different formats of spreadsheets, is it possible to create a spreadsheet that cannot be mapped and understood by spreadsheet disambiguation technology?

The answer is absolutely yes. It is certainly possible to create a spreadsheet that does not conform to the "standard" spreadsheet format *and* does not correspond to the simple list format.

This type of spreadsheet cannot be used for the purpose of automatically transforming data into a corporate database. Of course, it is always possible to manually transcribe a spreadsheet, however tedious and onerous a task that might be.

A Spreadsheet in a TXT Format

While converting from an .xls file to a .pdf file is not typically recommended, it is possible to change extensions to other common formats. For example, changing extension from .xls to .txt is a perfectly acceptable option. When a spreadsheet is converted to a .txt format, the xlstab, linefeed, and eold special characters are preserved.

In Summary

The unique name for a spreadsheet comes from the system designation. Any report name found on the spreadsheet is unreliable. Some spreadsheets are organized into "books" that are made up of multiple sheets.

A spreadsheet can contain all sorts of special characters and special features. However, for the purpose of corporate databases, the most important special characters are xlstab, linefeed, and eold.

If desired, entire sections of a spreadsheet can be blocked off.

In addition to the "standard" spreadsheet format, there is also the simple list format.

It is true that a spreadsheet can be formatted so that it cannot be automatically managed by spreadsheet disambiguation software.

On occasion it is desirable to place a spreadsheet into .txt format. A .txt format is a perfectly acceptable choice when it comes to spreadsheet disambiguation since special characters are reserved in the .txt format.

A spreadsheet can contain all sorts of special characters and special features. However, for the purposes of corporate databases, the most important special characters are — blank, linefeed, and null.

If desired, entire sections of spreadsheet can be blocked off.

In addition to the "standard" spreadsheet format, there is also the [illegible] format.

It is true that a spreadsheet can [illegible] so that it cannot be automatically managed [illegible] disambiguated [illegible]

[illegible] A [illegible] special characters [illegible] in the [illegible] format.

6: Spreadsheet Disambiguation

Transforming spreadsheet data into a corporate database format is called *spreadsheet disambiguation.* Spreadsheet disambiguation consists of both process and technology that combine to produce the transformation. The process of spreadsheet transformation is divided into several distinct steps. Each of the steps will be described here.

SELECTING SPREADSHEETS FOR INCLUSION INTO CORPORATE DATA

The first step in the process of spreadsheet disambiguation is selecting the spreadsheets for processing. Most spreadsheets will never be suitable for serving as a basis for corporate data. In order to evaluate whether a spreadsheet is fit to be changed into corporate data, the analyst must answer questions including:

- How reliable is the data on the spreadsheet?

- Is the data on the spreadsheet in a standard format? If not, can it be reformed into a standard format?

- Is the data on the spreadsheet something that is of use across the corporation? To multiple organizations?

- Is the data on the spreadsheet regularly updated or kept current?

- Is there a clear owner (or manager) of the data in the spreadsheet?

- Is there another very similar set of data being collected elsewhere?

- How often are new values added to the spreadsheet?

- How often are the values on the spreadsheet changed or reconfigured?

- Are the values found on the spreadsheet well understood and used often?

Once spreadsheets have been selected for transformation into corporate data, the next step is to consider the frequency of update. How often will the spreadsheet be submitted for inclusion into corporate data? As a rule, data that changes frequently is not a good candidate for corporate data. The more stable the data, the better corporate data it will create. Typically an update frequency of weekly to monthly is common.

The third consideration is identification of the source of the spreadsheet. If a spreadsheet does not have a clear and consistently identifiable owner, then the spreadsheet is not a good candidate for inclusion. The owner can either be an individual or a department.

It becomes obvious that most spreadsheets are not good candidates for inclusion in spreadsheet disambiguation. For a variety of reasons, most spreadsheets are disqualified.

RECASTING THE SPREADSHEET

Once a spreadsheet is selected for transformation into corporate data, the owner of the spreadsheet is notified. If the spreadsheet is not in the form of a "standard" spreadsheet or a simple list, then an investment of time is made to recast the spreadsheet into that format.

Remember: it is not absolutely mandatory that a spreadsheet be in standard form. But if a spreadsheet is *not* in that format, then the costs of processing the spreadsheet escalate.

LOGGING THE SPREADSHEET FOR TRANSFORMATION

The next step in the transformation process is logging the spreadsheet in. It is at this point that the physical ownership of the spreadsheet passes from the original owner to the organization that is charged with data transformation. Upon transferring the spreadsheet, the spreadsheet is "logged in".

As mentioned earlier, the information gathered during the logging process includes:

- Identifying the name of the spreadsheet

- Identifying the date and time the submission was made

- Identifying who submitted the spreadsheet

- Identifying any other relevant information – the size of the spreadsheet, the language the spreadsheet is in, any restrictions, etc.

The login process is very important in the transformation of spreadsheet data to a corporate database, as it represents one of the vital links in the establishment of data lineage.

ENTRY INTO THE PATH QUEUE

The next step in the transformation process is the entry of the spreadsheet into the path queue. The path queue is the location in the computer where the spreadsheets that are to be processed are held. For the most part, the entry into the path queue is a mechanical act. If there needs to be a change of extension types, the change is usually made here, before the spreadsheet is entered into the path queue.

DEFINING THE SPREADSHEET HEADINGS

The next step is to tell the system where the headings of the spreadsheet are. This is achieved by selecting the heading or headings from the spreadsheet and placing this definition into the ssdef table. Note that if there already exists a heading definition in the ssdef table, then this step is unnecessary.

PAIRING THE SSDEF SPECIFICATION TO THE SPREADSHEET

The next step is to run the spreadsheet through the disambiguation technology. In order to use the spreadsheet disambiguation technology, all prior steps must have been followed carefully. The spreadsheet disambiguation can only commence after loading the spreadsheet into the path queue and loading the ssdef table. If the ssdef heading definitions match properly with the spreadsheet, then a "pairing" occurs. This means that the spreadsheet is ready for the identification of all the column names and all the row identifications.

If by chance there is not a successful pairing, it means that the ssdef heading definitions have not been made properly. In this case, the analyst must return to the previous step and try again.

If you get a result of an unsuccessful pairing, you may be annoyed at first. In fact, the failure may be a useful thing. It can alert you to changes that have been made to the spreadsheet since the last time it was run through spreadsheet disambiguation, and help you keep your heading definitions up to date.

FINDING AND CREATING DATABASE DEFINITIONS AND VALUES

Once a spreadsheet has been paired with its appropriate ssdef heading definition, the next step is to read the spreadsheet and to create database definitions. The ssdef heading definitions ensure that the column headings can be distinguished from ordinary line items on the spreadsheet. In addition, the ssdef definitions ensure that the correct column names will be appropriate and ready for each value that needs to be processed.

In this step, the spreadsheet is read and each value on the spreadsheet has its context identified. The output from this step is a simple database that lists all the data found on the spreadsheet.

THE INTERMEDIATE DATABASE

The output from the previous step results in the creation of what is termed the "intermediate database". For all practical purposes, the intermediate database is a working database that is not meant to hold the final output of corporate data. In a way, the intermediate database holds "raw" data.

The data held in the intermediate database serves as input for two different functions. One of those is the creation of the mnemonic database, which holds strictly metadata. The second is the actual corporate data. The mnemonic database holds the metadata that was pulled from the spreadsheets, while the corporate database holds the actual values of data from the spreadsheets.

SOME ANOMALIES

At this point, most of the processing and data should be familiar to the reader. However, there are some processes that have not yet been discussed, as they are not considered "mainline" processing. These include:

- EXCLUSIONS – On some spreadsheets it is necessary to specify entire areas of the spreadsheet that need to be excluded from disambiguation processing. In these cases, the exclusion areas of the spreadsheet are defined.

- DISPLAY DISTINCT COLUMNS – When database output is collected, it is possible for the same value to be read from the spreadsheet more than once. It is useful to see when duplicate values have been collected.

- AUTOMATED SSDEF CHECK – Under normal circumstances, a spreadsheet is paired with definitions on a one-on-one basis. Occasionally, though, it is useful to load a lot of spreadsheets into the path queue and let the system try to automatically pair the ssdef data to the spreadsheets.

- DUPE SSDEF VERIFICATION – It is possible for identical ssdef specifications to be entered into the ssdef table. When this happens, there may be confusion in processing against the ssdef table. It is worthwhile to conduct an independent audit of the ssdef table to make sure that the entries into the table are unique.

After the intermediate database is defined, the output is sent to the *final output* database. A certain amount of editing is required as data makes this transition.

See Figure 6.1 for a summary of these anomalies plus examples from prior sections.

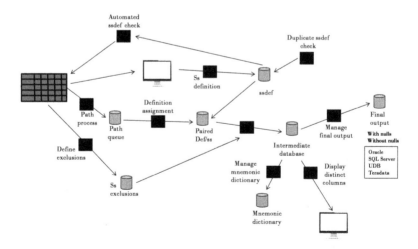

Figure 6.1: One implementation of the infrastructure to turn spreadsheets into corporate data

Later chapters will discuss the transfer of the intermediate database into the final output database. For now, there are a few more important issues to address in the creation of corporate data from spreadsheet data.

WHAT IF AN ERROR IS DISCOVERED?

What happens when an error in a spreadsheet is discovered? First off, it is absolutely normal for occasional errors to be discovered. So it is not surprising that this issue should arise.

In almost every case the procedure for dealing with an error in data is to correct the error in the spreadsheet and then rerun the processing depicted in Figure 6.1. It rarely makes sense to go into the infrastructure to fix the error after processing has commenced. In other words, the time to correct a spreadsheet error is at the moment the spreadsheet is populated with data, not after the spreadsheet has begun its journey into corporate data.

In almost every case, the amount of time required for processing is so small that it simply makes more sense to erase all the processing that has occurred for the spreadsheet and rerun the processing with corrected numbers.

MANUAL EFFORT REQUIRED

Let's return again to the issue of how much manual effort is required in spreadsheet disambiguation. It goes without saying that the less manual effort required, the better. Minimizing the manual effort speeds the process and reduces the chance of human error.

When considering the spreadsheet disambiguation processing (as summarized in Figure 6.1), there really are two kinds of manual interventions that are encountered. One manual intervention is the simple triggering of a process once the data is ready and in place. This manual intervention is inescapable, and is not prone to errors.

The second type of manual intervention is one that does require some amount of thought and skill. The only place where this intervention occurs is where the ssdef specifications are made. Unfortunately, there is no way around manual intervention here.

SPREADSHEET WIDTH

One issue that sometimes arises is that of spreadsheet width. A spreadsheet can be defined so that it is very, very wide. A spreadsheet that is too wide can go beyond the boundaries of the technology that reads and manages the spreadsheet. In terms of managing an oddly shaped spreadsheet, if the spreadsheet is *too* wide it can cause the disambiguation process to malfunction.

SUBDIVIDING A SPREADSHEET

In almost every case, a spreadsheet can and should be processed just as it was created. However, on rare occasion it is necessary to split a spreadsheet up into multiple spreadsheets and to process these subdivided spreadsheets individually, processing each "page" in this "book" of spreadsheets.

No Value for a Column Name

Another circumstance that needs to be accounted for is what happens when there is no value under a column name. Such an occurrence is fairly common.

There are at least two ways to handle this circumstance:

1. If no value is present, define a null value (such as "NULL").

2. Simply omit the column name and value from further processing. In this case there are no mentions anywhere of the column name.

Neither of these options is preferable over the other. The selection of one or the other option depends entirely on the nature of the data. In some circumstances, one option is preferable; in other circumstances the other option is preferable.

No Column Headings

Another common occurrence is a spreadsheet with rows of data and no column headings. Again, there are at least two ways to handle this circumstance:

1. Artificially create column names

2. Specify each value with its own ordinal specification

Creating the ssdef Specification Once

A final consideration is that of the creation and management of ssdef specifications. As illustrated in Figure 6.2, only the first occurrences of identifiers in a spreadsheet need to be defined into the ssdef table. All subsequent iterations of the same spreadsheet can use the previously-defined ssdef specifications—as long as there are no changes.

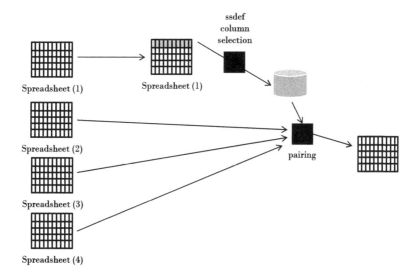

Figure 6.2: When multiple spreadsheets of the same type are run, only the first spreadsheet needs to have the columns defined

IN SUMMARY

At a high level, spreadsheet disambiguation is the process of ingesting a spreadsheet and turning that spreadsheet into corporate data.

The process starts with the selection of spreadsheets as candidates for corporate data. Most spreadsheets are not good candidates for inclusion into corporate data.

The next step is to log the spreadsheet in for processing.

The next step is the inclusion of the spreadsheet into the path queue.

Next comes the definition of the headings into the ssdef table.

The next step is the pairing of the ssdef specification with the spreadsheet. This step is a useful "self-check" for determining whether changes have been made to the spreadsheet since the last iteration was processed.

The next step is the running of the spreadsheet disambiguation technology. In this step, the values from the spreadsheet are paired up with the context of the values. The context of the values is determined by finding the column name and the row identifier.

The spreadsheet disambiguation process is used to build the intermediate database. The data from the intermediate database serves as a basis for two files — the *final output* of corporate data, and the mnemonic database.

Some of the considerations in the processing of the spreadsheet data into corporate data are:

- When to correct erroneous data?

- What to do about columns that are devoid of values?

- What to do about lists that have no column names?

7: The Intermediate
Database

The output of spreadsheet disambiguation is a database called
the intermediate database. For all practical purposes the
intermediate database is a "working" database. It is not
expected that the intermediate database hold actual corporate
data. Instead, the data found in the intermediate database is
data that is held in abeyance, awaiting further processing.

FINDING ERRORS

One value of the intermediate database is that if errors are
found in a spreadsheet, and if the errors need to be corrected, it
is relatively simple to destroy the intermediate database and
recreate it.

The intermediate database gives the organization a "second
chance" at creating valid corporate data.

In addition, the intermediate database gives the analyst a "sand box" to play in, where data can be easily created and recreated without having to commit to a final format.

A third value of the intermediate database is that it creates a place where several spreadsheets can be processed together and where the merger of the spreadsheets can be considered without having to make a commitment to the final corporate database.

In short, the intermediate database gives the organization a lot of flexibility in its movement from spreadsheet data to corporate data.

THE CONTENTS OF THE INTERMEDIATE DATABASE

The contents of the intermediate database are simple. They are derived from reading and interpreting the spreadsheets that have been paired.

The elements of data that are found in the intermediate database include:

- The spreadsheet system name (in order to specifically identify the spreadsheet that was the source of the processing)

- The row identifier

- The column name

- The value lifted from the spreadsheet

- The date processed

FUNCTIONS SERVED BY THE DATA ELEMENTS

The data found in the intermediate database serves a variety of functions. Lineage is preserved by including the spreadsheet name and date processed. If necessary, any value that has been processed can be traced back to a specific spreadsheet and a specific date.

The context of the value that has been lifted includes the row identifier and column name. The row identifier and the column name combine together to specifically describe a value in "real world" terms.

And, of course, there is the value itself, as lifted from the spreadsheet.

These elements combine to start the basis for corporate data. Figure 7.1 illustrates the different types of data elements found in the intermediate database.

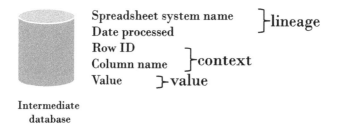

Figure 7.1: Types of data in the intermediate database

ALTERNATE NAME

There is one other element that can be added to the existing data derived from the spreadsheet. That element is called the "alternate name".

It is optional to add an alternate name; it has no necessary connection to the spreadsheet. Strategically, though, alternate name is very important.

There are many reasons why including an alternate name is strategically important. The first is that if you lift data from multiple spreadsheets, you'll likely find that there is no coordination of the naming conventions used by different organizations. It is expected that when data arrives at the intermediate database, it arrives with a multitude of name structures.

It is very useful, though, for the organization doing the data management to have all their spreadsheets similarly named. The alternate name allows this coordination to take place.

As an example, the name "MONTHLY ACCOUNTABILITY STATEMENT" is lifted from one spreadsheet. From another spreadsheet the name "ACTIVITY AMOUNT" is lifted. Both of these are alternate names for the spreadsheet.

Now, when the end user analyst looks at the data, it's clear that they're looking at the same element of data—despite the fact that in different spreadsheets the data elements are called something very different.

A second (but related) issue that is resolved by alternate names arises from interface with existing operational data. The alternate name can be chosen so that the new values are consistent with values already found in the corporate database. By coordinating the alternate name value with existing corporate data names, the job of the analyst is made much easier.

Figure 7.2 shows that there is great importance placed on the usage and assignment of alternate name.

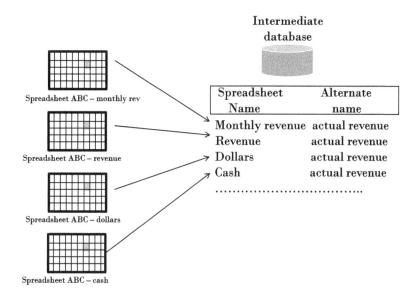

Figure 7.2: The alternate name is important!

ADDING CONTEXT TO DATA VALUES

It has been established that raw data values taken from a spreadsheet have no context. As such, data without context is hardly fit to be entered into a corporate database. It is only after disambiguation that the data values are fit to be entered into a corporate database.

EDITING DATA IN THE INTERMEDIATE DATABASE

As data is prepared to be entered into the final corporate database, there is one more step to complete: to edit out undesirable data.

It is normal for a spreadsheet to contain lots of types of data. Some of that data is vital, but other data on the spreadsheet may be of little or no importance. Data that is of little or no importance merely "clutters up" a database. Data of specious value makes more important data hard to find and use.

Therefore, it is a standard practice to "weed out" some data elements in the intermediate database. There are lots of ways to filter out the undesirable data. One way is to merely identify data that is desirable and delete everything else. Another way is to filter data with certain metadata characteristics.

This "weeding" process can be accomplished either automatically or manually, depending on the spreadsheet data.

Beyond editing, there are many other tasks that can be accomplished with the intermediate data. The data can be counted, compared, restated, and more. Because the intermediate database is not final data and can be easily and quickly recreated, it serves as a "working" database.

IN SUMMARY

The processes of spreadsheet disambiguation produce a working database known as the "intermediate database". The intermediate database consists of the following elements:

- Spreadsheet system name

- Row identifier

- Column name

- Value

- Date of processing

- Alternate name (optional)

The intermediate database is a working file. It can be edited, have data deleted, have alternate names added, and so forth. The alternate name allows disparate data elements to be grouped together. In addition, the alternate name allows for a bridge for other corporate data to be created.

The intermediate database serves as a basis for further processing.

8: The ssdef Database

As we've discussed, the ssdef database (or table) is the place where all spreadsheet heading definitions are stored. The headings are brought into the ssdef table by means of a module that displays the headers, which then allows the headers to be selected.

The ssdef table is internal to the spreadsheet disambiguation application. There is little or no use for the ssdef table outside the spreadsheet disambiguation application.

ORGANIZING DATA INSIDE THE SSDEF TABLE

The ssdef table can be arranged in one of two basic manners. The first arrangement is by individual column names. In this arrangement, only one column name at a time is stored. In order to determine what the header line looks like, the line must be reconstructed, a column name at a time. This is often referred to as the "individual column" method.

The second way the ssdef table can be structured is by the capture of the entire line, where all of the column names are captured at once. This is referred to as the "composite column" method.

PROCESSING USING SSDEF RECORDS

Again, the sole purpose of the ssdef file is to hold spreadsheet header definitions, which are then matched against a spreadsheet. As mentioned earlier, a match must be an *exact* match.

Once a match to a spreadsheet is made, the system knows how to recognize a header line on the spreadsheet. Once the header line is recognized, the system can tell the difference between a header line and the other lines in the spreadsheet. Using that information, the system can then read the spreadsheet and determine the context of each value on the spreadsheet.

SEARCHING THE FULL PATH QUEUE

Usually the pairing process is carried out on a limited basis. This means that a single spreadsheet is paired (or not) with a record of heading definitions found in the ssdef table.

However, it is possible to search the entire path queue rather than looking for a hit on just one spreadsheet. Doing a full path queue search can save a lot of time when processing many spreadsheets.

One more note on the ssdef table: it is generally a fairly simple table. However, on occasion, it is worthwhile to verify that no duplicate records have been entered into the ssdef table. If duplicate records find their way into the ssdef table, there can be a confusion of processing, especially when searching the full path queue. To avoid that confusion it is wise to occasionally scan the ssdef table to ensure that no duplicate records have been inadvertently entered.

In Summary

The ssdef table is the place where spreadsheet column name definitions are stored. The ssdef table can be organized on a column name-by-column name basis, or by a single inclusion of the entire heading line.

As a rule, the pairing process is conducted between one spreadsheet and one ssdef table. However, it is possible to compare one ssdef table against *all* entries in the path queue.

9: The Corporate Database

Throughout the book so far, we've been discussing how to go about using data from spreadsheets to create a corporate database. At this point, we've thoroughly examined every step in this process, and it's finally time to take a look at the end result: the corporate database.

The corporate database is the result of the spreadsheet disambiguation process. The data that comes out of spreadsheet disambiguation is a "working" database called the intermediate database. It is this intermediate database that serves as the basis for input into the corporate database.

The corporate database can be created in whatever database format is desired. Typical database formats include Oracle, SQL Server, UDB/DB2, Teradata, and others.

Data in the corporate database has different properties than data found in other corporate data stores. Corporate data originating from spreadsheets has a premium placed on data lineage, and a secondary emphasis on the veracity of the data.

This emphasis on lineage over veracity is a necessity because of the very origins of the data itself. If a value is questioned, the rigorous attention paid to lineage allows that value to be traced quickly and concisely back to the spreadsheet that generated it.

FROM INTERMEDIATE DATA TO CORPORATE DATA

There are several functions involved in processing the intermediate database into the corporate database. Certainly the main objective is to move intermediate data into the corporate database. But another function is the removal of some intermediate data. Not all data stripped off of a spreadsheet is useful in the corporate world. The spreadsheet may contain irrelevant or extraneous data that only clutters up the corporate data. Unwanted intermediate data is filtered out now, before it gets to the corporate database.

Another important function is establishing an alternate name for some of the data flowing into the corporate database. Establishing an alternate name for some corporate data allows for the consolidation of names coming from disparate spreadsheets, and for conformance to the names used in other corporate data. Examining existing corporate data is a good way to determine what the alternate name ought to look like.

GROUPED CORPORATE DATA

The corporate database derived from spreadsheet data has one important characteristic that sets it apart from other corporate data not derived from spreadsheet data. The data found in the corporate database derived from a spreadsheet is not separated by subject area.

As an example, it might be normal to find dollar amounts, product classifications, and shipping quantities all in the same corporate database.

In other corporate data, it is customary for data to be organized and grouped according to its application.

For this reason, it may be useful to further separate corporate data into more finely refined groupings of data.

TRACING THE LINEAGE

The lineage of corporate data should be easily and accurately discerned. The entire infrastructure of spreadsheet processing supports the ability to trace the lineage of corporate data, as shown by Figure 9.1.

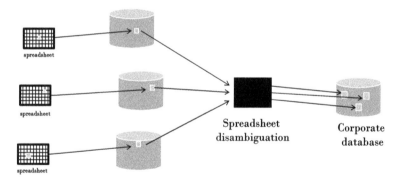

Figure 9.1: Lineage of corporate data

IN SUMMARY

The corporate database is fed from the intermediate database. The corporate database can be in any standard database format, including Oracle, SQL Server, UDB/DB2, Teradata, and more.

Data can be edited as it passes from intermediate data to corporate data. In addition, an optional data element, an alternate name, can be added.

Data in the corporate database is not grouped by subject area. In order to be compatible with other corporate data, it may be useful for group corporate data by subject area.

At any moment in time, it is mandatory that the lineage of corporate data be open and obvious.

10: The Mnemonic Dictionary

While the primary purpose of spreadsheet disambiguation is to extract context and values from spreadsheet data, there is another valuable byproduct. The process allows the creation of a data dictionary of terms that are found on the spreadsheets. The dictionary that contains these terms can be called the "mnemonic dictionary".

The purpose of the mnemonic dictionary is to catalog the metadata that is found on all the spreadsheets that participate in corporate data. The mnemonic dictionary is concerned *only with metadata* from spreadsheets that are destined for corporate data. On the other hand, the corporate database is concerned with both context *and* values of this data.

THE CONTENTS OF THE MNEMONIC DICTIONARY

The contents of the mnemonic database are very similar to the contents of the corporate database. The contents of the mnemonic dictionary include:

- Spreadsheet system name

- Line name/number

- Column name

- Row identifier

- Alternate name (optional)

- Created by

- Created date

- Description (optional)

The mnemonic dictionary, again, does not contain values. Instead, the mnemonic dictionary contains both lineage and metadata. Some data elements in the mnemonic dictionary can be considered both lineage *and* metadata elements at once.

GROUPING LIKE DATA ELEMENTS

One of the many uses of the mnemonic dictionary is in grouping together related data elements. This is especially useful when looking across multiple spreadsheets.

In general, there are two components that are gathered for each record of metadata: the row identifier and the column name.

These two elements come from different places in the spreadsheet, and are combined to define a single value of data.

One way that different mnemonics of data can be related (and potentially combined) is through similarity of the column names, as illustrated in Figure 10.1.

Jan	revenue
Feb	revenue
Mar	revenue
Apr	revenue
....	....

Figure 10.1: Related elements with different spreadsheet names

The other way that data in the mnemonic dictionary can be related or combined is through similarity of the row identifier, as shown in Figure 10.2.

Net profit	9/15/07
Net profit	9/30/07
Net profit	10/15/07
Net profit	10/30/07
....	....

Figure 10.2: Related elements with different spreadsheet names

A third possibility for relating and combining different mnemonic dictionary elements is to use the alternative name to combine completely unrelated elements of data. Figure 10.3 shows this possibility.

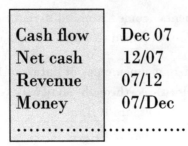

Cash flow	Dec 07
Net cash	12/07
Revenue	07/12
Money	07/Dec

Figure 10.3: Related elements with alternate names

APPLYING NAMING CONVENTIONS

When building the mnemonic dictionary, there is an opportunity to start applying meaningful naming conventions. When a spreadsheet is built, there is rarely much thought given to naming conventions. Furthermore, when a spreadsheet is being built, it's not common to consider what other organizations have named things. Every organization is different, and every organization is free to name spreadsheet items however they wish. There really are no standards or conventions for naming spreadsheet data.

However, when it comes to using the alternate name, the organization can enforce whatever naming standards and conventions it wishes.

VALUE OF THE MNEMONIC DICTIONARY

There are many reasons why the mnemonic dictionary is a valuable resource to the organization. The best way to describe the value of the mnemonic dictionary is to state that the mnemonic dictionary serves as a road map to the spreadsheet data found in the corporation. It can be seen as a decoder to understand the data in many different spreadsheets throughout the corporation. Remember, though, that the mnemonic dictionary only serves to catalog the spreadsheets destined for the corporate database.

IN SUMMARY

The mnemonic dictionary is of particular value to the analyst community. The mnemonic dictionary is a natural starting point to finding data that is stored on spreadsheets.

In many ways, the mnemonic dictionary is a natural extension of the corporate data dictionary. The corporate data dictionary applies to *all* sorts of data in the corporation, while the mnemonic dictionary applies *only* to spreadsheet data. Nevertheless, the mnemonic dictionary plays a complementary role to the corporate data dictionary.

The mnemonic dictionary holds metadata as does the corporate data dictionary. The difference is that the metadata found in the mnemonic dictionary comes from spreadsheets, whereas the metadata found in the corporate data dictionary comes from sources other than spreadsheets. However, both the mnemonic dictionary and the corporate data dictionary hold metadata.

11: Political Considerations Within the Organization

While the transformation of spreadsheet data into corporate data is certainly a technical exercise, the organizational and political considerations are important as well.

SHIFTING CONTROL

The most impactful of these considerations is the shift of data control. As long as data is in a spreadsheet, the data is under the direct control of the end user. IT has no say or no consideration of the data found in a spreadsheet. After all, one of the primary reasons why the spreadsheet rose in popularity was the end user's desire to have control.

But as the data moves through the transformation process that has been described, there is a shift in the control of the data.

When the data arrives in the corporate world, the data is firmly in the control of the organization's IT department.

There are many implications of this change in control. When data was in the control of the end user, data was:

- Managed directly by the end user

- Easily changed whenever the owner desired

- Fairly private, as only a few people had access to (or even knew about) the spreadsheet

But as the data moved to the control of IT, the data was suddenly:

- Managed by procedures and design

- Regularly and dependably available

- Widely accessible

- Much more credible

Clearly, the nature of the data itself changes dramatically as control passes from the creator to the corporation.

IMMUTABILITY OF DATA

As data moves across the political landscape, several technological changes occur. However, the data maintains a certain degree of consistency, recognizable wherever it exists across the landscape. The database may change, the spreadsheet may change, the procedures managing the data may change, and the people viewing and using the data may change...but there is always a common thread. The aspects of this common thread that make the data recognizable in all steps of the process include:

- System spreadsheet name

- Column name

- Row identifier

It is these three contextual elements that remain consistent throughout the data's lifetime.

THE IMPORTANCE OF ALTERNATE NAMES

This "common thread" of consistent information is very important across the political landscape. But as data enters the realm of IT and corporate data, there is another element that becomes of paramount importance: the alternate name. The reason why the alternate name takes on special meaning in the IT environment is twofold:

1. The alternate name can be controlled, whereas the names of other data cannot be.

2. Alternate names can be used to link spreadsheet data to existing corporate data.

In many ways, the alternate name becomes like the Rosetta stone of data elements. It is the key to using common terminology to link spreadsheet data and corporate data.

By linking spreadsheet names to existing corporate data names, the job of the analyst is made much simpler.

LIMITED EDITING

For the most part, data that comes from the spreadsheet environment remains just as it was found. As it enters the corporate world, though, some small amount of editing is acceptable. These types of editing include:

- Tolerance edits, where a numeric value is between 1 and 10, for example.

- Simple numeric edits, as in changing the European number 2.350 to the American form of 2,350.

- Standard acronym edits, like changing Texas to TX and New Mexico to NM.

Note that with these simple edits, the meaning of the data is not changed.

SUPER CLASSIFICATIONS OF DATA

One useful practice in data management is to use the alternate name to form *super classifications* of data. A super classification of data fits multiple occurrences of spreadsheet data.

As a simple example of a super classification of data, consider the data element *monthly revenue*. There may be any number of ways that a spreadsheet portrays monthly revenue. The super classification of data encompasses all of those different spreadsheet definitions.

The super classification of data elements becomes a component of the mnemonic dictionary.

THE LINEAGE OF CORPORATE DATA

We've already seen that the lineage of spreadsheet data is of paramount importance. One of the interesting questions that arises is that of lineage and corporate data. It is certainly true that spreadsheet data has lineage. Lineage of data is the essence of spreadsheet data. But does corporate data also have lineage?

The answer is yes, of course corporate data has lineage. However, lineage of data is of a secondary concern with corporate data. With corporate data the veracity of the data – the correctness of the values of data – is the major concern. But it is certainly true that corporate data originating outside of spreadsheets has lineage.

RELATIVE VOLUMES OF DATA

One important question we haven't asked yet is this: how much spreadsheet data is there? There certainly may be any volume of data associated with spreadsheets. However, the volume of spreadsheet data pales in comparison to the volume of data found in "standard" corporate data. Depending on the corporation and the circumstances, there may be ten times the order of magnitude of corporate data than of spreadsheet data.

IN SUMMARY

As data shifts from spreadsheets to corporate databases, the control of the data shifts from the end user to the IT department. With the shift in control comes a change in autonomy, discipline, accessibility, and other aspects the data.

Data is consistently recognizable across the transformation components by the three following elements:

- Spreadsheet system name

- Column name

- Row identifier

As data passes into the corporate data environment, it is possible to do some light editing that does not change the value of data.

Alternate names can be used to create super classifications of data.

From a volumetric standpoint, there is typically *much* more "standard" corporate data than there is spreadsheet data.

12: Data Modeling and the Spreadsheet Environment

The subject of data modeling has long been discussed in books, articles, and conference presentations. This will be a very cursory discussion on the subject for which much more in-depth material is written elsewhere.

The data model represents an abstract way of looking at data. This abstraction is very useful when dealing with the enormity and complexity of corporate data. There are different levels to the data model.

THE ENTITY RELATIONSHIP DIAGRAM

At the very highest level is the entity relationship diagram, or ERD. The ERD identifies the major subject areas of the corporation. The different subjects connect through relationships. The relationships describe the business logic binding one subject to another.

The ERD does not purport to show any great level of detail. Instead, the ERD shows major categories of data and how those categories relate to each other. A simple ERD is depicted in Figure 12.1.

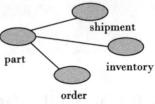

Figure 12.1: A typical ERD

THE DATA ITEM SET

Each subject area has its own subset of more detailed information. This more detailed description of the subject area can be depicted in a separate diagram called a *data item set*, or *DIS*. The DIS describes in much greater detail the characteristics of the entity that it portrays. Some of the things found in the DIS include:

- The key, or major identifier of data for the subject area

- Attributes about each subject area

- Grouping of the attributes

- Foreign keys, or relationships to other subject areas

Figure 12.2 on the next page shows a DIS.

THE PHYSICAL MODEL

From the DIS is created a physical rendering. The physical rendering of the DIS includes such things as:

- The physical characteristics of the attributes

- Indexes

- Order of attributes

- Degree of uniqueness

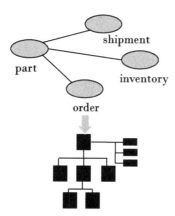

Figure 12.2 Each entity has a data item set, or DIS.

Figure 12.3 shows a physical rendering of a DIS.

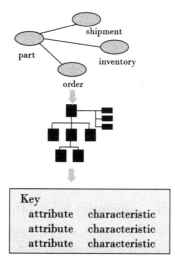

Figure 12.3: Each grouping of data within the DIS has a physical model

THE DATA MODEL

Together, these three structural components form the corporate data model, as shown in Figure 12.4.

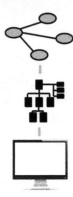

Figure 12.4: The data model

THE DATA MODEL AND SPREADSHEET DATA

When it comes to spreadsheets—and especially to spreadsheet data that is destined to become corporate data—the data model for this kind of data is the same as the data model representing any corporate data. However, there is one major difference in the role of the data model as it relates to spreadsheet data and as the data model relates to corporate data. When there is a difference between the data model and spreadsheet data, the data model is adjusted. In the case of corporate data, when there is a difference between corporate data and the data model, corporate data is adjusted.

There is an underlying assumption behind this subtle difference: in spreadsheet data, the owner of the spreadsheet is always correct. (Or at least, if the spreadsheet is not correct, only the owner can go back and make corrections to the spreadsheet).

However, with corporate data, if the data is found to be wrong, then the designer of the systems that manage corporate data can go back and make corrections to the corporate data.

This is a subtle but very important difference between spreadsheet data and "standard" corporate data, and the data models that represent each.

"CORRECTNESS" OF DATA

There really are two aspects to the "correctness" of data. One aspect is the accuracy of the data value. For example, if the number "7" should be the number "9," that data value would be considered inaccurate.

The other aspect to the correctness of data is the structural correctness of data. This is an issue when in one spreadsheet, the vehicle identification number is the one the manufacturer designates. In another spreadsheet, the vehicle identification number is the shipping number used in transport of the vehicle. The problem is not necessarily that these two numbers are different, but that these two numbers have a different significance.

ALIGNING DATA FROM DIFFERENT SPREADSHEETS

The modeling of spreadsheet data gives rise to another important question: what if two (or more) spreadsheets have a difference in the significance of data that should be closely aligned?

Furthermore what if there *must* be a resolution of the numbers? In some cases resolution is not important. Differences can be overlooked. Or differences can simply be ignored. As an example of the case when a number can be ignored, suppose the results of a football game were being discussed. The spreadsheet says that the score was 35-14 in favor of Dallas. In fact the score might have been 35-21. As long as the winner is recorded correctly, the exact score is not of a great concern (except perhaps to a bookmaker).

But in other cases, structural differences between data *cannot* be ignored. In such a case, how can a resolution be made?

There are lots of possibilities when it comes to resolving data differences. The easiest option is to find the data that appears to be misinterpreted, and replace it with data that is a better match. When such a substitution is a possibility, then the solution is easy and obvious.

But what if there is no easy and obvious resolution? Some suboptimal solutions are described below.

AN ALGORITHMIC RESOLUTION

When two (or more) values *must* be aligned, then one option is to introduce an algorithmic solution. In the algorithmic solution, data from one spreadsheet is taken and algorithmically recalculated into the form of the other spreadsheet. However, it is not always possible to find an algorithmic solution.

AN INDEXED RESOLUTION

As a final resort, there is always the indexed solution. In the indexed solution, the data from one spreadsheet is collected. The data is then aligned with data from the second spreadsheet. Then an index is created that allows a cross reference to be made between data in the spreadsheets.

It takes a lot of work to create an indexed solution. Tying the elements of data together is usually not an easy thing to do. But an indexed solution is always a possibility, in the worst of cases.

RESOLUTION AND THE DATA MODEL

Furthermore, however inconsistencies are resolved, the method of resolution becomes a part of the data model. Figure 12.5 shows that the means of resolving the differences between two (or more) types of data belongs in the description of the data model.

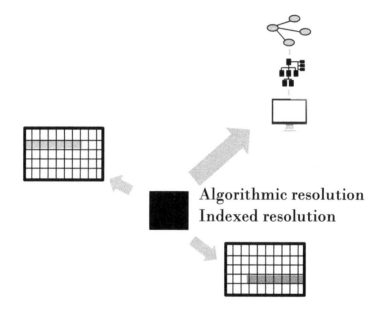

Algorithmic resolution
Indexed resolution

Figure 12.5: The resolution becomes part of the spreadsheet data model

There is another important use of the data model for spreadsheets. Data models come in handy when data from the spreadsheet is headed for a data warehouse.

SPREADSHEET DATA IN THE DATA WAREHOUSE

It has long been known that raw data entering a data warehouse needs to be transformed. In this regard, data coming from a spreadsheet is no different.

Why, though, should data coming from a spreadsheet be transformed? And doesn't transforming the data change the value of the data? And isn't the owner of the spreadsheet the only person that is allowed to change the value of data?

The answer is this: for the purposes of preparing spreadsheet data for a data warehouse, transformation *does not* truly violate the principle that only the owner of the spreadsheet should be allowed to change data.

In order to see why this is true, consider an example.

Suppose the owner of a spreadsheet enters a value of 135 Mexican pesos. Suppose the spreadsheet is transformed into a data warehouse, but the data warehouse keeps track of money in US dollars. As the data from the spreadsheet is written into the data warehouse, the transformation from Mexican pesos to US dollars is made. 135 Mexican dollars is equivalent to $10 US dollars, using the exchange rate at the time. So the value $10 US dollars is written into the data warehouse.

Now suppose it is found that the value of 135 Mexican pesos is found to be incorrect; it should have actually been 674 Mexican pesos. Only the owner of the spreadsheet can make that correction.

When data is sent into a data warehouse, the original data is not changed. Only the owner of the spreadsheet can change the original data. However, the transformation process of entering the data warehouse can change the form of data as desired, but not the basis for the transformation.

CHANGING SPREADSHEET DATA

Can data from a spreadsheet be changed, then? It all depends on the nature of the change. As discussed earlier, light editing is generally fine. Similarly, if the change is for the purpose of entering a data warehouse, then spreadsheet data changes are permissible. But dramatically altering the original values of the data is typically not recommended.

IN SUMMARY

The data model is an abstraction of the data found in a system. The standard data model has three levels: the ERD level, the DIS level, and the physical level.

The model for spreadsheet data is the same as the model for standard corporate data, with one significant difference. When spreadsheet data and the data model differ, changes are made to the data model. In the case of corporate data, when the data model differs from corporate data, the corporate data is changed.

What if data from two or more spreadsheets need to be aligned? A simple method of resolution is to choose different data. An alternative is to algorithmically resolve the data, if possible. If no other solution works, disparate values can always be resolved through the creation of an index.

However the resolution is achieved, the resolution itself needs to become a part of the data model.

Changing data on spreadsheets is an important subject. Changes to spreadsheet data that involve light editing or data warehouse transformations are acceptable. But changes to the original source data should only be carried out by the owner of the spreadsheet.

13: Case Study

There is nothing like an example to reinforce new concepts that have been discussed, so let's examine a case study. Consider the following sample spreadsheet, taken from some financial projections.

	Range of LTV ratios at originatio	Aggregate outstanding principal	% of Total	Number of accounts	% of Total
0% - <5%		£96,336.23	0.01%	10	0.10%
5% - <10%		£1,326,013.95	0.11%	54	0.54%
10% - <15%		£3,541,422.98	0.30%	135	1.36%
15% - <20%		£5,329,808.20	0.45%	150	1.51%
20% - <25%		£8,771,649.11	0.74%	206	2.07%
25% - <30%		£11,792,864.37	1.00%	232	2.33%
30% - <35%		£17,057,425.93	1.45%	284	2.85%
35% - <40%		£19,983,208.43	1.69%	277	2.78%
40% - <45%		£25,532,065.68	2.16%	328	3.30%
45% - <50%		£29,238,228.10	2.48%	346	3.48%
50% - <55%		£39,030,646.00	3.31%	410	4.12%
55% - <60%		£61,328,687.59	5.20%	570	5.73%
60% - <65%		£53,167,437.61	4.51%	468	4.70%
65% - <70%		£55,917,800.93	4.74%	491	4.93%
70% - <75%		£154,715,374.68	13.11%	1,118	11.23%
75% - <80%		£128,091,495.43	10.86%	967	9.72%
80% - <85%		£109,790,543.15	9.30%	783	7.87%
85% - <90%		£228,519,061.87	19.37%	1,584	15.91%
90% - <95%		£210,990,331.28	17.88%	1,422	14.29%
95% - <97%		£15,167,011.54	1.29%	114	1.15%
97% - <100%		£540,099.23	0.05%	4	0.04%
>=100%		£-	0.00%	-	0.00%
Total		£1,179,927,512.29	100.00%	9,953	100.00%
	Range of LTV ratios at end of re	Aggregate outstanding principal	% of Total	Number of accounts	% of Total

Figure 13.1: Financial spreadsheet

The header line is found in row 2. The remaining rows on the spreadsheet contain actual data. The first step is to send the spreadsheet into the disambiguation software. This step is shown in Figure 13.2. The spreadsheet is identified by the system spreadsheet name.

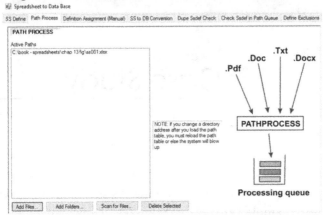

Figure 13.2: Processing with disambiguation software

After the spreadsheet is selected, it will be displayed as in Figure 13.3.

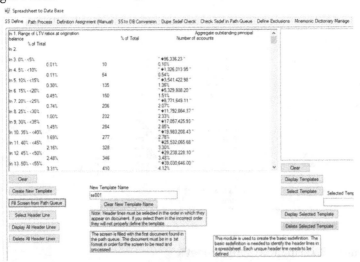

Figure 13.3: After disambiguation

After the spreadsheet is displayed, the next step is to identify and select the header(s) in the spreadsheet. In Figure 13.4, it is evident that the header has been selected.

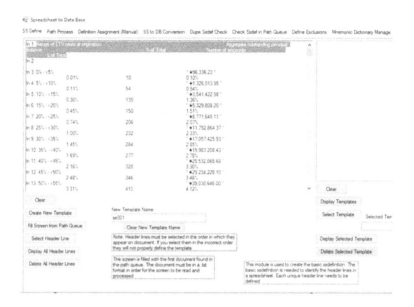

Figure 13.4: Selecting the header

After the header line has been selected, the next step is to pair the header line with the spreadsheet, as shown in Figure 13.5.

Figure 13.5: Pairing the header line with the spreadsheet

Once the pairing of the spreadsheet and the heading definitions occurs, the next step is the actual creation of the intermediate database, which is illustrated in Figure 13.6.

Figure 13.6: Creating the intermediate database

Once the intermediate database has been created, the next step is the creation of the mnemonic dictionary. This step is optional, and is shown in Figure 13.7 on the facing page.

Once the mnemonic database has been created, the next step is to create the final output from the intermediate database. Note that null values are created in this version of the final output, as seen in Figure 13.8 on the facing page.

Figure 13.7: Creating the mnemonic dictionary

Figure 13.8: Creating the final output

However, it is not necessary or even desirable to show null values in every case. Figure 13.9 shows the same output data with null values removed.

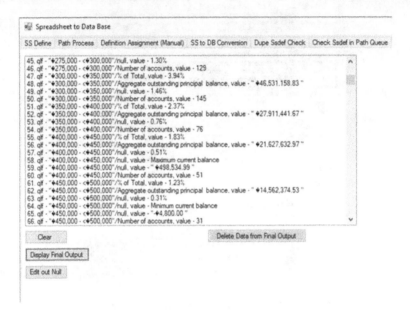

Figure 13.9: Final out without null values

It is of interest to note that all of these steps, from the identification of the spreadsheet to the output of corporate data, took less than one minute to complete.

Glossary

Attribute – a value of data that is distinguishable from other values

Cell of a spreadsheet – a basic unit of data found in a spreadsheet

Column – a vertical table in which values are selected from the same domain

Column name – the name of a column in the spreadsheet

Comments – a field of data containing free form text

Context – the surrounding environment that gives definition to a word

Data dictionary – a repository of the metadata useful to the corporation

Data element – an attribute belonging to an entity

Direct access of data – the ability of a database management system to directly find data, as opposed to having to sequentially search for it

Logical data model – a data model based on inferred relationships

Mnemonic dictionary – a dictionary of terms found on a spreadsheet

Multiline row – a row in a spreadsheet where the row id name is the same

Record – a unit of data that typically contains keys and attributes

Recurring spreadsheet – a spreadsheet that is issued on a scheduled basis

Reporting – the process of collecting data from various sources and presenting it to business people in an understandable way

Requirements – a statement of what is needed in the functionality of a system

Spreadsheet – the primary tool found in personal computing

Spreadsheet book – multiple spreadsheets that have been grouped together

Spreadsheet disambiguation – the technology that reads a spreadsheet and merges values and context

Spreadsheet exclusion – the practice of ignoring entire sections of a spreadsheet because those sections are used for general purpose reporting

Spreadsheet external view – the view of the spreadsheet seen as the spreadsheet is printed on paper

Spreadsheet Hell – the condition an organization finds itself in when it has many, many spreadsheets and no believability of the data found on those spreadsheets

Spreadsheet internal view – the view of the spreadsheet as it look to the computer

SQL – the language interface for relational systems

SQL Server – the DBMS built and managed by Microsoft

ssdef file – the system file used to store spreadsheet header definitions

xls – the extension for Excel spreadsheets

xlstab – the separation special character found in spreadsheets

Index

Accuracy, 10, 20, 21, 38, 42, 101

Accuracy rate, 21

Adobe, 43, 46

Algorithmic resolution, 102

Algorithmic solution, 102

Alignment, 44

Alternate name, 71, 72, 73, 74, 75, 82, 84, 86, 88, 93, 94, 96

Analysis, 6, 41, 51

Analyst, 19, 23, 27, 33, 34, 35, 50, 51, 57, 61, 70, 72, 89, 93

Anomalies, 3, 62

Asset, 6

Attributes, 98, 99, 113, 114

Audit, 10, 63

Automated, 8, 19, 20, 21, 40, 41

Automated ssdef check, 63

Autonomy, 1, 8, 9, 10, 95

Backup, 9

Blocks, 51

Books, 2, 3, 4, 11, 28, 48, 49, 54, 65, 81, 97, 114

Business environment, 6

Calculations, 7, 9

Catalog, 85, 89

Categories, 98

Cell, 2, 21, 22, 23, 25, 39, 113

Cell formula, 21, 25, 39

Cell metadata, 39

Character, 28, 29, 30, 31, 43, 44, 45, 49, 55

Classical corporate systems, 3

Colors, 49

Column heading, 22, 23, 31, 32, 35, 36, 37, 41, 45, 50, 51, 53, 61, 66

Column name, 22, 23, 24, 25, 34, 36, 39, 40, 41, 45, 46, 50, 53, 61, 66, 68, 70, 71, 74, 77, 78, 79, 86, 87, 93, 96, 113

Columnar heading, 36

Comments, 113

Common thread, 92, 93

Complexity, 6, 19, 97

Concepts, 3, 21, 47, 107

Context, 3, 21, 22, 24, 34, 36, 39, 40, 41, 44, 50, 52, 61, 68, 71, 73, 78, 85, 113, 114

Contextual data, 40

Corporate data, 1, 3, 4, 10, 11, 12, 13, 14, 17, 18, 19, 20, 21, 23, 24, 27, 30, 34, 35, 36, 37, 38, 39, 40, 41, 43, 44, 46, 47, 50, 52, 54, 55, 57, 58, 59, 60, 62, 64, 67, 68, 69, 70, 71, 72, 73, 75, 81, 82, 83, 84, 85, 86, 89, 91, 93, 95, 96, 97, 100, 101, 105, 112

Corporate data model, 100

Corporation, 2, 6, 11, 13, 14, 15, 58, 88, 89, 92, 95, 97, 113

Correctness of data, 101

Corrupt, 9

Cost differentials, 20

Cross reference, 102

Data dictionary, 85, 89, 113

Data elements, 7, 71, 72, 74, 75, 84, 86, 93, 94, 113

Data exchange, 2

Data item set (DIS), 98, 99, 105

Data line, 40, 60, 81

Data model, 97, 100, 101, 103, 105, 114

Data modeling, 97

Data reliability, 13

Data values, 7, 73, 101

Data warehouse, 103, 104, 105, 106

Database, 7, 18, 30, 36, 37, 41, 61, 62, 63, 68, 69, 73, 74, 77, 81, 82, 83, 85, 92, 113

Database definitions, 61

Database design, 7

Database formats, 81, 83

Database output, 62

Date, 37, 59, 61, 70, 71, 74, 86

Date processed, 70, 71

Degree of uniqueness, 99

Delimited, 28

Delimiter, 45

Demarcation, 28, 29

Descriptors, 22, 24

Development, 5, 6

Diagrams, 6, 98

Directory, 47

Disambiguation, 57, 60, 62, 65, 73, 77, 81, 108

Disambiguation software, 108

Display distinct columns, 62

Double blank, 45, 46

Dupe ssdef verification, 63

Editing, 63, 73, 74, 94, 96, 105, 106

Elements, 3, 24, 70, 71, 72, 74, 86, 87, 88, 93, 96, 103

End of line (eold) character, 29, 31, 33, 34, 41, 44, 49, 54, 55

End user, 1, 2, 4, 5, 6, 7, 8, 9, 10, 11, 27, 34, 35, 36, 41, 72, 91, 92, 95

Entity relationship diagram (ERD), 97, 98, 105

Error, 64

Exclusions, 62

External, 27, 28, 30, 32, 33, 41, 44, 114

External view, 44, 114

Externally, 27

Filter, 74, 82

Folder, 47

Foreign keys, 98

Formal, 2, 16, 17, 18, 23, 24, 34, 38

Formal spreadsheet, 16, 23, 34

Formality, 16

Format, 2, 7, 16, 28, 29, 30, 34, 35, 36, 41, 43, 44, 45, 46, 52, 53, 54, 55, 57, 58, 59, 70

Formula, 16, 22, 39

Graphics, 49

Grouped corporate data, 82

Header, 40, 51, 77, 78, 108, 109, 115

Header line, 40, 51, 77, 78, 108, 109

Heading definitions, 37, 60, 61, 77, 78, 110

Hex 0x09, 28

Hex 0x0A, 29

Hex 0x0D, 29

Identifier, 23, 24, 31, 33, 34, 35, 47, 48, 71, 98

Immutability, 92

Index, 99, 102, 105, 117

Indexed resolution, 102
Indexed solution, 102, 103
Informal, 15, 16, 17, 34
Informal spreadsheet, 16, 34
Infrastructure, 63, 64, 83
Intercompany communication, 17
Inter-corporate communication, 17
Intermediate database, 62, 63, 68, 69, 70, 71, 72, 73, 74, 75, 81, 82, 83, 110
Internal, 17, 18, 27, 28, 29, 30, 31, 32, 33, 34, 36, 40, 41, 43, 44, 46, 52, 53, 77, 115
Internal view, 27, 28, 29, 30, 31, 32, 33, 36, 43, 44, 53, 115
Internally, 27, 28, 30, 34
Interpretation, 7, 16, 21, 33
Intersection, 41
IT, 1, 5, 6, 7, 8, 10, 11, 91, 92, 93, 95
IT development process, 11
IT labyrinth, 5, 6
Iteration, 16, 68
Key, 46, 93, 98
Language, 60, 115
Legacy system, 6
Liabilities, 2, 6, 9
Library, 2, 37
Lineage, 3, 11, 37, 38, 39, 42, 71, 82, 83, 84, 86, 95
Linefeed, 29, 31, 33, 34, 41, 44, 49, 54, 55
Linefeed character, 29, 31
Log, 37, 38, 42, 67
Logged in, 37, 42, 59
Logging, 37, 59
Logic, 39, 97

Mainframe, 8
Malfunction, 65
Management, 2, 3, 9, 10, 11, 12, 66, 72, 94, 113
Manipulate, 6, 34
Manual, 18, 19, 20, 40, 41, 64, 65
Manual effort, 64
Manual intervention, 40, 41, 65
Mechanical process, 21
Metadata, 23, 36, 39, 62, 74, 85, 86, 89, 113
Metadata characteristics, 74
Methodologies, 6
Microsoft Excel®, 2, 28, 29, 43, 115
Missing column heading, 31
Missing value, 32
Mnemonic database, 62, 68, 86, 110
Mnemonic dictionary, 85, 86, 87, 88, 89, 94, 110, 111, 114
Mnemonics, 87
Multiline row, 33, 114
Multiple sheets, 49, 54
Naked number, 21
Naming conventions, 72, 88
Non-recurring, 15, 16, 24
Non-recurring spreadsheets, 15, 16, 24
Non-standard spreadsheet, 52
Null, 66, 110, 112
Null value, 66, 110, 112
Numeric value, 94
Omit, 66
Operational data, 72
Optical character recognition (OCR), 45, 46
Optional, 23, 72, 74, 84, 86, 110

Oracle, 81, 83

Ordinal specification, 66

Organization, 3, 4, 6, 7, 8, 9, 35, 59, 69, 70, 72, 88, 91, 92, 114

Output, 61, 62, 63, 68, 69, 110, 111, 112

Owner, 38, 48, 58, 59, 92, 100, 104, 106

Pairing, 60, 61, 68, 78, 79, 109, 110

Path queue, 60, 61, 63, 68, 78, 79

Personal computer, 1, 8

Photos, 49

Physical characteristics, 99

Physical rendering, 98, 99

Political, 91, 92, 93

Political considerations, 91

Private data, 15

Processing, 7, 10, 36, 37, 38, 42, 57, 59, 62, 63, 64, 65, 66, 67, 68, 69, 70, 74, 75, 78, 79, 82, 83, 108

Public data, 13, 14, 17

Raw data, 73, 104

Real world, 39, 71

Reconfigured, 58

Record, 38, 78, 86, 114

Recurring, 15, 16, 17, 18, 24, 114

Recurring spreadsheets, 15, 16, 17, 24

Relationship, 39

Relative volumes, 95

Reliable, 3, 9, 46, 47, 48, 57

Report, 48, 49, 51, 54

Report name, 48, 49, 54

Reporting, 51, 114

Requirements, 5, 6, 114

Resolution, 101, 102, 103, 105

Restrictions, 60

Road map, 88

Row identifier, 22, 23, 24, 25, 31, 33, 34, 35, 36, 39, 40, 41, 45, 50, 52, 61, 68, 70, 71, 74, 86, 87, 93, 96

Self-check, 68

Shift, 91, 95

Shortage, 2, 12

Significance, 101

Simple list, 52, 53, 54, 55, 59

Simple list structure, 53

Simple numeric edits, 94

Size, 60

Source, 37, 38, 42, 58, 70, 106

Special character, 28, 29, 30, 34, 41, 43, 44, 46, 49, 54, 55, 115

Specifications, 36, 67

Spectrum, 16, 17, 24

Spreadsheet data, 3, 4, 10, 11, 12, 13, 14, 19, 24, 27, 36, 37, 38, 39, 42, 44, 57, 60, 68, 70, 74, 82, 85, 88, 89, 91, 93, 94, 95, 96, 100, 101, 103, 104, 105, 106

Spreadsheet disambiguation, 3, 39, 40, 41, 53, 54, 55, 57, 59, 60, 61, 64, 65, 67, 68, 69, 74, 77, 81, 85, 114

Spreadsheet disambiguation technology, 53, 54, 60, 68

Spreadsheet exclusion, 114

Spreadsheet formatting, 47

Spreadsheet hell, 8, 9, 10, 12, 114

Spreadsheet name, 37, 48, 71, 87, 93

Spreadsheet processing log, 37

Spreadsheet structure, 35, 52
Spreadsheet width, 65
SQL, 81, 83, 115
SQL Server, 81, 83, 115
SSDEF database, 37, 77
SSDEF heading definition, 61
SSDEF Specifications, 63, 65,
  66, 68
SSDEF Table, 39, 41, 50, 51, 60,
  61, 63, 67, 68, 77, 78, 79
Standard acronym edits, 94
Standard corporate data, 105
Standard format, 35, 36, 52, 53,
  58
Storage, 2, 10, 24
Strategic, 72
Subdividing, 65
Subject area, 82, 84, 97, 98
Summary, 11, 24, 41, 46, 54, 63,
  67, 74, 79, 83, 89, 95, 105
Super classifications, 94, 96
System identifier, 48
System name, 47, 48, 70, 74, 86,
  96

System spreadsheet name, 48,
  93, 108
Table, 36, 63, 77, 78, 79, 113
Teradata, 81, 83
Terminology, 47, 93
Time, 1, 2, 5, 9, 15, 16, 19, 20,
  35, 37, 45, 59, 61, 64, 77, 78,
  81, 84, 104
Tolerance edits, 94
Tracking, 2
Tradeoff, 9
Transcription, 21
Transferability, 7, 17
Transformation, 11, 17, 18, 19,
  20, 21, 30, 36, 37, 50, 57, 58,
  59, 60, 91, 96, 104
Transformation log, 37
UDB/DB2, 81, 83
Undesirable data, 73, 74
User requirements, 7
Veracity, 3, 10, 11, 13, 81, 82, 95
Weeding, 74
Working database, 62, 74
xlstab, 28, 29, 31, 33, 34, 41, 43,
  44, 45, 49, 50, 53, 54, 55, 115